Memories of Alec
&
Our Intercultural Marriage

Alec's family.

Memories of Alec
&
Our Intercultural Marriage

by Ursula Blank-Chiu

Design & production: Kerrie L. Kemperman

ISBN-13: 978-0-692-90969-0

Printed in the United States
10 9 8 7 6 5 4 3 2 1

In memory of Alec,

for our children and grandchildren

ACKNOWLEDGMENTS

Kerrie L. Kemperman has followed and advised this story with much patience and experience. The writer, age 92, feels deep joy and gratitude for Kerrie's dedicated devotion to the task.

Monica, Marcel, and Michael Chiu were fine editors who helped me remember important points of our family story.

Dr. Annette White-Parks is a dear friend and served as an early reader of many of these stories.

TABLE OF CONTENTS

Three generations of the Chiu family, 1951 (Alec, bottom right).

INTRODUCTION

The following stories from Alec's life represent significant events and reflections that he often repeated in conversations with me, with his family, and in wider circles. They are the memories that upheld or depressed his mind while moving from Mainland China to Hong Kong, from Taiwan to Japan, and to America.

I first heard these tales as a fellow immigrant student and friend in Chicago, and eventually as his wife. I imagined, questioned, and reasoned with him, always wondering how he integrated so many contradictory experiences into his well-structured daily life. I brought along my own insights and experiences from my childhood in Germany, and shared them with him.

He also shared these stories with his children, often with imaginative extensions and diversions. At times, he wove portions of his life story like vines into the tenets of philosophy as Alec illustrated abstract concepts of philosophy for his students. His reflections on how to survive from one day to the next led him, eventually, away from the question of how to sustain and manipulate business economics to asking, "What is it all about? What is the meaning of life in Eastern, as well as in the Western imagination?"

His listeners were rarely aware that his tales and thoughts were sustained within a weakened body caused by the pain of *Spondylitis Ankilosis,* a progressive spinal inflammation that his physician presumed was genetic. Like a Buddha, he bore it all with a gentle smile. Like a hermit, he escaped into silence and books. Yet, he also created laughter and shared the comical and the contradictory that he noticed so often.

His storytelling was not just entertainment, but a mirror: to who he was and what held him firmly anchored in his life. Even more than his daring stories, his joy of teaching and his exploration of meaning captivated me. Alec so enriched my life that I eventually felt urged to write his story, in loving memory.

Did I always understand and reflect his meanings? If my goodwill failed, the reader should know that my life was conditioned by Western culture. Yet, our marriage was creative and alive to the end. We had the patience and loving will to accept each other in our differences.

CHAPTER 1

BEGINNINGS IN CHINA

On March 10, 1934, Alec Chiu was born Kwai Fang Chiu, the second son of a traditional Confucian family, in Taipei, Taiwan. The details presented here are what Alec shared with me.

In the 1920s, Alec's parents had left their homeland of Taiwan (which at that time was part of China) so that his father could complete his education at a business and trade school in Tokyo, Japan, while his mother worked in a sushi bar and maintained the family finances. Their native languages were Mandarin and Haka, but they both became fluent in Japanese while living in Japan. After Mr. Chiu completed his studies, the couple moved to the outskirts of Shanghai, China, where they started a weaving business. Mainland China's economy was prosperous at that time. Their factory became successful and well respected, producing sturdy cloth for farming clothes and material for panama hats.

In 1930 the birth of their first child, a son, Raymond, brought hope for the extension of the family name. According to Confucian customs, he would be responsible for taking care of his elderly parents. When Quai Fang (Alec) was born four years later, he also was joyfully welcomed. As the second-born son, he would not inherit the family business but neither would he have the obligation to provide for his elderly parents.

In the late 1930s, political tensions developed when the Chinese government protested the occupation of Manchuria by Japanese military forces. Although the rest of the world paid little attention to these initial transgressions, international awareness increased in 1937 when Japanese armies poured from Manchuria into China. In short succession, Peking, Shanghai, and Nanking came under Japanese occupation. For the Chiu family, this meant not only constant threat from fighting between Mao Tse-tung's Red Army and Chiang Kai-shek's Nationalist forces vying for power inside China but also submission, in the end, to the superior Japanese forces.

According to Alec, the Japanese allowed his father's business to continue operating normally at first, but later was forced to produce nothing but cloth for Japanese military uniforms. For the Japanese, this reduced the cost of uniforms and sped up the process since they didn't have to import the cloth from Japan. Alec did not remember whether only the cloth was produced or whether the uniforms were stitched by seamstresses in the factory.

The days of Alec's early childhood were not peaceful or without threat from the occupation. He remembered taking the bus to his elementary school one day when low-flying Japanese planes strafed the fields with machine guns. The children jumped from the bus and lay flat in the ditches, trembling, until the roar of the planes faded away. Alec admitted, "I wet my pants in fear, and was so ashamed."

From year to year, increased insecurity and anxiety over-shadowed the family's daily life and their interactions with the Japanese. When news spread that Nanking, the nearby capital, had suffered the indiscriminate murder of hundreds of thousands of civilians and tens of thousands of women raped, the fear became more immediate. Nanking was less than 200 miles from the Chiu home in Shanghai.

Kids in elementary school soon learned about these violent events and feared the possibility of these cruelties in their environment. The Japanese had imposed severe food rationing on the Chinese population, and even the allotted food quantities often arrived in spurts only. Kids had to contribute their share to feed the family and helped as harvest laborers. They spent weekend days gathering potatoes in the wide unprotected fields.

"I was always afraid of another attack by planes," Alec told me as an adult. "I do not like to eat potatoes for my memory retains that I saw, ate, and feared gathering too many of them at that time." He and his brother found the peanut harvest less exhausting, but the potato harvesting had to be done, even in place of school.

Alec remembered unusual ideas for food gathering, such as pulling out fish from a pond that was drained gradually. When hundreds of fish were flopping in the soft mud, the kids could grab them with their bare hands. Their mother was happy when Raymond and Alec brought home the slippery, squirming catch of the day.

Birds also became an extra meat supply. Alec said that his gang of boys hung bags of thin mesh on the top of large poles. The bags, conical in shape with small holes at the end, expanded when it was windy, inviting birds to fly inside but they would be unable to escape through the other end. His mother was quick to prepare small bird morsels for meat supply in a dish. Bird bodies contain only small meat portions, but Chinese dishes are sparing of meat and more generous in vegetable fillers. Also vegetables were easier and quicker to grow on the small piece of land that his father owned.

Food deprivation must have been severe, judging from Alec's frequently told story in which he reported, "One day, after a dinner with more meat than usual, I asked my mother, 'What kind of meat did you use in this dish?' She hesitated, with a peevish expression on her face, then said, 'I caught the big rat in the shed, the one that scared you sometimes,' then she looked away when I started making gagging noises. Did she tell the truth or was she just teasing me? I wonder to this day."

A combination of events led the Chiu family to leave Shanghai. Alec remembered his father's worried questioning, "What will happen to us when the Japanese are defeated? The Chinese will accuse us of having been collaborators with the enemy. We speak Japanese, and we produce enemy uniforms. Nobody will believe that we did this under duress." Both sons understood that the family followed Chiang Kai-shek, leader of the Nationalist party, politically. But how would they defend themselves if Mao's Communist party gained power after the Japanese left?

From their father, they knew that they were far from being farmers. "We are not peasants," Alec's father often said; "We are landed business owners who will be persecuted by a Communist government. If they gain political power, even our own factory workers will become our enemies."

In 1945, a few months before the defeat of the Japanese and the end of World War II, the family left Shanghai, abandoning the factory buildings and a two-story home, carrying only the essentials. Alec was eleven years old. For him, the loss of his shepherd dog, left behind at the factory, was like the loss of a faithful friend.

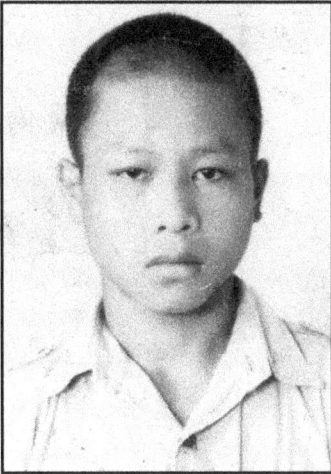

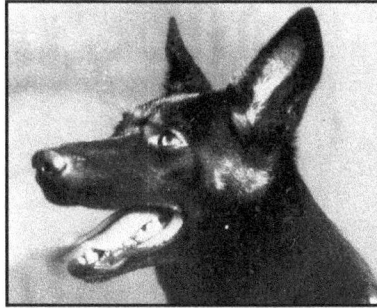

Alec and his beloved shepherd dog.

CHAPTER 2

ALONE IN HONG KONG

Alec remembered very little about the trek from Shanghai to Hong Kong, the southernmost Chinese business center. Along the route, his father searched for a new mainland Chinese location for his weaving business, but in the end, he chose to live under the Chinese-British administration of Hong Kong. This former British colony still had its own legal system, finances, police power, and international delegates. It had remained in close contact with several Western trading posts. The British-style education system also appeared advantageous for the Chiu children. However, the city had experienced major upheavals and radical changes during the war. From 1941 until 1946, the Japanese kept a tight and cruel occupancy of the community, which had reduced the population to half of its pre-occupation numbers. War, hunger, sickness, and emigration had contributed to this decline.

When the Chiu family arrived in Hong Kong, British rule had been reestablished. The flood of immigrants from China, trying to escape Communist rule, had become a big problem for the health and accommodation of the new settlers. Living spaces were extremely difficult to get, but Alec's father had a friend who found an apartment for the family on the outskirts of town, close to a middle school for Raymond. For Alec, this family friend, a dentist, offered a space in his own house, which was close to the elementary school.

"It was not really a room," Alec said, "but a space in a hallway, between two rooms, just wide enough to place two boards, one for a bed and the other for a desk. There was no window, no direct access to the outside. During the day, I stayed at school as long as I could, studying in the library or joining soccer practice outdoors."

Alec's prowess as a soccer player quickly won him companions at his new school, as well as ribbons for leadership. The school, St. Joseph's Elementary, was run by nuns in the style of the British education system. Morning and night, he walked up or down on the steep hill leading to the upper level island, where St. Joseph College was located. He rarely had money to use the tram that ran between the two levels of the city.

Contact with his host family was very limited. Alec was permitted to cook for himself, but it rarely happened. However, when allowed, he made himself busy at the dentist's lab, even filing one of his own teeth into shape when it gave him trouble.

"Visits with my parents during that year in Hong Kong were rare due to the distance and my school requirements. Their absence left a deep loneliness in my heart." Alec explained. The loneliness became even worse when his parents left Hong Kong to resettle in Taiwan, taking Raymond with them. His father's business connections were too limited to grant the support he needed to operate a factory in Hong Kong.

Alec's teachers were aware of his absent family and his longing to be reunited with them. In his photo collection, several pictures show him somewhat gloomy, but he appears radiant with friends or when displaying a sports trophy or celebrating Christmas.

In the course of time, Alec worried over how he could make faster progress learning the English language. He was ambitious and wanted to follow classes taught in English as well as those taught in Mandarin. Realizing his efforts, Sister St. Peter said to him, "Kwai Fang, if you want to improve your English, I am willing to help you." He was quick to accept her offer, and they began lessons using an English grammar book and the Catholic Catechism as texts. Her teaching was consistent and very helpful, and he made even faster progress when he started keeping company with some of his native English-speaking classmates. As to memorization, in this case the basic tenets of Catholic religion, he was well disciplined and successful, just as he had been when memorizing the characters for the Chinese Mandarin language.

At the end of the year, Sister St. Peter said, "Your English is much improved, your grades do you honor, you know your Catechism. Do you want to be baptized into the Catholic faith now?"

BAPTIZED! He had never thought of that! Alec debated the issue in his mind. It would help him to become a member of the large group of Christian students and he could participate in their celebrations. He thought maybe it was wise to accept some guidelines to live by since he was far away from his family. Later, when telling this story as an adult, he would explain that the Chinese, due to their Confucian rules for living, are accustomed to accepting and strictly following rules and written guidance.

Alec agreed to be baptized, and Sister St. Peter was pleased. During the baptismal ceremony he chose his Christian name, Alec, which he has used ever since. His brother, Raymond, had been given an English name at birth, so Quai Fang figured he should have an English name too. From then on, Alec followed the rule of attending church every Sunday, and confessing his shortcomings regularly.

Several months later, Alec met his religion teacher, a priest, who asked, "Which church are you attending?" Alec replied proudly, "The red building around the corner, with the large tower," and then watched the priest's smile change into an expression of confused amazement.

"Alec," he replied, "Do you realize that all this time you have gone to services at the Lutheran Church? From now on make the right choice. Go to the Convent Chapel, or let me show you a Catholic church closer to your home. From there you should worship God from now on."

Oh, well, Alec thought. He had done his best so far. He also needed to practice soccer, get good grades in his classes, and participate in a fifty-member harmonica club. He decided that after all of these things, he would try his best to visit the correct church.

CHAPTER 3

HOME IN TAIWAN

Alec was not the only family member who had been heavy-
hearted with the family separation; his parents were also sad
and concerned with his living so far away. After he had spent
two years in the Hong Kong school system, Alec's parents
brought him back to their new home on the island of Taiwan.

As Alec prepared to leave Hong Kong at the end of sixth
grade, his classmates were quick to tease him about his new
home. "Watch that you don't fall off 'the sweet potato,'" they
said, referring to the shape used to describe the island by its
first Portuguese immigrants. Another comment warned, "Alec,
you might be swallowed by 'the largest whale in the ocean,'"
another description of Taiwan preferred by early fishermen.

Alec researched his future home and found, indeed, that
it was only 245 miles in length and 90 miles in width. If he
was disappointed about his small-island living, he might have
read that Portuguese sailors who visited the island in 1544
named it *Ilha Formosa,* "Beautiful Island," a name it retained
until the Japanese occupied the Republic of Formosa in 1895.

The Chiu family were immigrants on an island established
by immigrants. Over the centuries the Portuguese, the Dutch,
and finally the Chinese had laid claim to this miniature island

in the ocean. The latter, as well as immigrants from Europe, confined its aboriginal inhabitants to eke out their living in the mountains. The eastern two thirds of the island from north to south with five high mountain ranges offered enough space, but little income with which to build their lives. Later, Alec would compare the fate of these indigenous peoples to that of the native tribes of the United States.

When the Japanese conquered the island in 1895 they named it Taiwan. Under their control, they brought it into the modern industrial world by creating transportation, sanitation, and public school systems. Rice and sugar cane production became major items for export. Hoping to bring culture to the "primitive island," the Japanese developed an elementary education system between 1936–1940, structured not only for their own children but also, in the end, for the Chinese, Taiwanese, and Aborigines. However, the discrimination between these groups did not easily disappear with education.

After the Japanese surrendered to the Allied Command in October 1945—the end of World War II—the army withdrew from Taiwan. An influx of Chinese business elites, intellectuals, and well-trained workers, all escaping Communism on the mainland, flooded in. In 1952, The San Francisco Peace Treatment would declare Taiwan an independent, self-governing nation.

While the Chinese, Taiwanese, and the Aborigines had the largest populations on the island, the Japanese had relegated them to the lowest status. Later, Alec would often mention childhood trips to Moon Lake in the mountains, where the family watched dance performances of the various aboriginal tribes.

Alec's parents had much to offer in the fast-progressing Taiwan: his father's education in Japan, their weaving trade in China, and fluency in Mandarin, Haka, Japanese, and English. Relatives and previous business connections, now refugees in Taipei, created favorable business opportunities for Alec's father.

According to Wikipedia, the Nationalist Chinese, fleeing to Taiwan, brought "the entire gold reserve, and foreign currency reserve from Mainland China. This unpredicted influx of human and monetary capital laid the foundation for Taiwan's later dramatic economic development."

It is not surprising that Alec's father gradually was able to expand his business to a larger scale, now that Mainland wealth entered Taiwan. Many of his former business relations in China had shifted to Taiwan. They, too, saw need for restarting the weaving machines for island-wide cloth production, and export. Along with his former business connections Alec's father approached new government agencies in Taipei for permits, acquired with the help of bribery and pay-offs. According to Alec, business progress was impossible without these political negotiations. With permits in hand, the expansion of the Chiu business was radical and swift.

Alec remembered his mother worrying about some rather tricky business ventures and lamenting, "Stop buying more property. We have more than we can handle already." Her husband and his two entrepreneurial partners created more and more business to produce more and more financial gain. Their gains increased when they realized the power of market manipulation. They bought cotton cheaply from China and held it, creating an artificial need on the national market, and then released the cotton at exaggerated prices. This business technique is considered fraudulent market manipulation in the United States.

CHAPTER 4

SCHOOL TROUBLE IN TAIPEI

Moving from Hong Kong to Taipei, Taiwan, was a joyous event for Alec. His father's business success meant that the family now owned a three-story house. Large warehouses, rental and commercial properties had been purchased in Taipei and Taichung. His father owned a Packard car with a metal figurehead on the hood, which Alec found very impressive. A chauffeur was hired since no self-respecting businessman in Taipei would drive his own car. Alec and Raymond were chauffeured to school, earning them much social status but also threatening gestures. A Chinese family with Japanese language skills and cultural experience had some advantages, but Raymond, and later, Alec, found that their physical safety was not always guaranteed. Japanese children could be unfriendly and aggressive; Japanese adults were especially hostile toward successful Chinese business owners.

The family's success and wealth relieved much of Raymond's concern about his future responsibilities toward his elders. He was a striving student and, now in high school, he loved to study English. He became an excellent writer and had some of his stories accepted for publication.

I remember that anytime Alec spoke of his brother, his comments were made with much admiration and affection. He would say, "While our parents were busy traveling to establish new business connections, my life felt safe under my brother's protection. He was always there to fend for me. At times we had to stay with relatives and Raymond was my center of stability and support. Our relatives were impersonal; we were just members of the bigger crowd. There was no excitement when we returned from school each day; no 'milk and cookie' treatment. Children need to feel appreciated and supported for their efforts."

Their parents soon acquired a second house nearby for Raymond and Alec to live in, with a maid to take care of their daily needs. The boys enjoyed a significant amount of freedom in their new lodging. Alec could bring his new shepherd dog home from its watch post at the cotton mill, leaving a second dog behind to guard the mill. The dog became a significant companion for him.

"During this time, my brother became my best friend and protector. He watched over my homework and defended me from teasing and attacks by older boys. We slept entwined and warm like cats when we moved into the big house on our own, under the care of a maid. Care-taking she did—cleaning, washing, and cooking—the rest was up to us."

Raymond became successful in all subjects at school whereas Alec's biggest success was in soccer, as head of the league. Since he liked to be popular, he often invited the team to their home. These gatherings included quiet games, eating and talking, certainly no homework or rough-housing. Alec said, "Our mother worried at times, but she had to follow Dad's desires to entertain business visitors and to take care of his needs. On weekends our parents often took us into the mountains or we spent time at the beach. It was then that they listened to our worries and wishes and needs."

Alec remembered clearly one instance of his father's generosity, "When I contacted him in a meeting to ask for money, he pointed to his back pocket from which I took his fat billfold, pulled a hefty amount from it, and put it back with his OK. Father was always generous with money, and also fun-loving and humorous when we had family time."

Alec's memory of the family's Chinese New Year celebrations was equally vivid. "There were many parties during the fifteen days of celebration. On the first day, the family honored the gods of Heaven and Earth. On the next day, the spirits of the ancestors were invited, as they were the foundation for the family fortune. I liked this celebration best because we could eat as many sweets as we wanted since they would secure a sweet year to come. There were also special dishes. I liked the meat-filled dumplings most of all and also the uncut noodles, which symbolized long life. Paper money—with wishes for a wealthy year—was exchanged on this day, along with baskets or crates of oranges for good health. The custom was to send the orange crates to the next relative as soon as they were received to avoid accumulation or over-purchase." I remember saying to Alec, "Don't we have a similar practice at Christmas, when we hand out surplus gifts of chocolate and fruitcakes to our own relatives or friends?"

One of the most depressing times of his years in Taipei happened during seventh grade. "I was not doing well academically because the transition from a British school system to a Chinese one was complicated and I could not fit my previous learning into the new curricula. It was only in soccer that I felt successful. The yearly final exams were dreaded by every student in my level, but mostly by me and a fellow student in the same situation. We thought that getting a pre-exam glance at the questions in the finals might save us. After more thought, the idea was translated into action and we found a way to get inside the school at night and then into the teacher's room. We located the exam questions in his desk and copied them, planning to review the answers the following day."

Alec used to tell this story with a mixture of daring pride and regret about the consequences. "I do not know who tattled on us, but we were not allowed to take the exams nor to return to school. Our parents were informed of our misdeed, which meant loss of face for them and the whole Chiu clan, a very serious event in Taiwanese society. It brings public humiliation and the devaluation of our family's social standing."

As always, when in need, Alec turned to his brother. Raymond would help him out of this dilemma. Sailing back to Hong Kong to St. Joseph's was the thing to do, Alec thought. Raymond agreed, and came up with the ticket and some money. Being too ashamed to tell his plans to their parents, Alec left them without farewell.

Alec (right) with classmates in Hong Kong.

CHAPTER 5

GREAT LOSSES AND IMPORTANT DECISIONS

Alec returned to his Catholic boarding school in Hong Kong, escaping the public shame of his bad decision in Taipei but not his regret at leaving his parents behind to cope with his wrong-doing and sudden departure. His father arranged for him to again stay at the dentist's home, where he had lived previously. After having a whole house in Taipei, it was hard to return to a simple hallway space without windows and two boards as furniture. He was sometimes allowed to cook for himself, but he had very little personal interaction with the family and he greatly missed his own.

Later in his life, Alec admitted, "This was a period of great loneliness and insecurity for me." His mind was now intently set on succeeding in his classes and showing that he could achieve in Hong Kong's British school system what had been impossible for him in Taiwan.

Gradually, news from home became less exuberant and confident. Although Alec's parents had not said much about the decline of their business, Raymond made occasional hints in his letters about business problems. Far from home, Alec could hardly imagine the realities of a bankruptcy. In his mind, his father was too clever and successful to lose his well-established empire.

Alec returned to Taipei at the end of eighth grade with an excellent report of achievement. With his graduation, he experienced joyous celebration of his achievements along with the sadness of farewells. The latter turned into shock when he discovered that the family's three-story house in Taipei was gone, along with the various shops and business buildings they had owned. The Packard automobile, with chauffeur, was being driven for a different owner.

The family now shared a modest apartment, and his father used a bicycle for transportation. His father's new business was peddling trinkets to former customers. Alec, a teen of fifteen, was deeply ashamed of his family's lowered social status, especially in front of former classmates and his soccer mates whom he had royally entertained in the past. His heart also went out in compassion for his mother, who all along had been fearful of the growth of business that led to her husband's overly bold ventures and eventual business collapse.

Beyond the material losses, there were still more decisive changes to come. According to Confucian tradition, the older son was destined to take over his father's business and to inherit his property. If the inheritance could support a second son, he would not have to worry, but Alec, the second son, now realized he would be on his own both to overcome the shame as well as to earn his own livelihood without family support.

Alec thought he might have a good chance to obtain a scholarship in Japan as a Chinese student since Japan had lost the war and owed reparations to China. Both of his parents had spent several years in Japan and spoke fluent Japanese, and had raised him and his brother to speak it as well. In spite of Sister St. Peter's tutoring, his fluency with the Japanese language was still stronger than his English. Alec wrote a letter to Father Thomas (who had forgiven his short adherence to the Lutheran faith in Hong Kong) asking for advice regarding his future education. Father Thomas quickly replied, and contacted the Marianist Brothers in Yokohama, Japan about the problem. Praising Alec's strong motivation, and his achievements in academics as well as on the soccer field, Father Thomas petitioned for a scholarship to Saint Joseph College in Yokohama, run by the Marianist Brothers. Although called a "college," it offered a high school level education. Father Wilhelm, the German director of the school, offered a four-year academic scholarship. Room and board would have to be eked out by Alec on his own. Elated by his good luck, Alec faced his parents and pleaded for a one-way ticket on a vessel from Taipei to Osaka, Japan, followed by a rail ticket to Yokohama.

Leaving home was difficult, but it was Raymond whom he would miss most of all. Raymond had been his protector and advisor during his childhood and teen years, during stints with relatives and classmates, or under the care of a maid.

"Raymond and I never fought, and I could rely on him in any trouble." Alec used to say. He admired Raymond for his intelligence and high honors in school. A high school senior at the time of Alec's departure, Raymond envisioned a college career in business so he could re-establish their father's trade even though his deeper interests were related to language, literature, and writing.

CHAPTER 6

STRUGGLES AND HUMAN KINDNESS IN JAPAN

"When the boat left the harbor of Taipei headed for Yokohama, the fall winds were not gentle," Alec would say, remembering his voyage to Japan with deep emotion. The upheavals in his life, his fear of the unknown, and the ever-changing rocking of the boat weakened his system and kept him in the cabin he shared with a dozen other passengers. He kept to his bed, as did several others. During calmer sailing, he finally dared to go on deck and sought out Chinese passengers he could ask about his destination. This was not an easy task because Chinese etiquette demands that younger people wait until elders and non-family members take the initiative toward conversation. The few Chinese teens he met were either "buttoned up" or not really acquainted with Japanese life and customs.

After three days of sailing they reached the Kyushu and Shikoku islands, where they were less exposed to the winds as on the open ocean. Freight was unloaded and reloaded in the harbors of Myazaki, where the boat anchored at each stop for a few hours but passengers were not allowed to disembark. On the last stretch toward Osaka, land was visible on both sides of the boat and Alec finally began to feel excited.

Alec knew about harbor traffic and confusion from living in Hong Kong, but—as he was to learn—there is little left to accident in a Japanese harbor. Once stepping off the landing bridge, well-marked pathways led the passengers to different control officers who directed them according to their nationality. Customs officers in neat uniforms, disciplined postures, and matter-of-fact expressions took each passport into their white-gloved hands and scrutinized photo identity and visa permits to enter the country.

"You are Chinese?" was the first question directed to Alec. "How old are you? What did you do in Taiwan and in Hong Kong? Why are you traveling to Japan? Can you show me your scholarship papers?" One question immediately followed the other; Alec felt their suspicion. He would experience this suspicion again and again during his time in Japan. "How glad I was that my skills in speaking Japanese did not fail me," Alec often said.

After thorough scrutiny of the papers from St. Joseph College, giving him the right to "occupy space in Japan," he was directed to pick up his luggage and present himself to a second customs officer. His single footlocker was thoroughly searched. Clothing, some books, and pictures of his family hid nothing and were hardly of political interest.

"Do you have any money on you?" the officer asked, closing the footlocker.

"Yes, I have Chinese currency to pay for my train to Yokohama."

"Let me see the money," was the command that followed his admission. Alec showed the bills and froze when he heard the ultimate verdict.

"No import of Chinese currency allowed. I have to confiscate your money."

After that, Alec hardly found the Japanese words to voice his horror.

"I have to pay for the train to Yokohama. I have to find my school. I have to eat on the way."

"No Chinese currency allowed," was the officer's unsympathetic reply.

"I have no friends or relatives in this country to help me," Alec almost shouted. "What am I to do without money?"

The officer already held the bundle of Taiwan dollars in his hand. He deposited the cash and turned to the next passenger.

There was Alec, fifteen years old, alone, penniless, in a foreign country. "I might as well jump into the ocean and disappear because there is nothing and nobody to help me," Alec thought. He could no longer suppress his heavy sobs and tears ran down his face. He stepped to the side not knowing what to do next when he heard an elderly Chinese gentleman ask the customs agent, "Officer, how much money have you confiscated from the boy?" He then turned to Alec, gave his name, and explained that he was a journalist who often traveled from Taiwan to Japan. "I am sorry for your difficulties and I would like to pay for your trip, so you can reach your school. Here is my address and the replacement of your money. If you can repay the loan, please do so. If not, then help somebody else when you can later on in your life."

As they walked together to the train, he explained to Alec that the Japanese—once masters of large parts of China and Taiwan now lost with their defeat—were rather hostile toward Chinese citizens and did not easily tolerate them in their country. "Do your best while you are here to show them that the Chinese are reliable and deserve respect," he cautioned me.

When they found the train station, the journalist took leave and disappeared into the crowd. "Gratitude for his compassion and generosity were now stronger in my heart than my shock and anger at the callous Japanese regulations," Alec recalled.

From St. Joseph College, he wrote to his father who repaid the money to the trusting and generous journalist. A thank-you note in Alec's hand accompanied this letter.

CHAPTER 7

AT ST. JOSEPH COLLEGE IN YOKOHAMA

On the train from Osaka to Yokohama, Alec had time to rethink the events of the last several days: his farewell from his depressed father, his protective older brother, and his mother, who cried and slipped her diamond-studded watch pendant into his pocket with the words, "In case you are in need, use this." The voyage at sea, with the shifting moods of the ocean waters, had absorbed some of the sadness of separation, but that had been followed by the rude interaction with the customs officer at Osaka harbor. How alone and threatened he felt in a hostile foreign world, an orphan without money. Only the Chinese journalist preserved his hope that his new school would be as compassionate as his generous benefactor had been.

Settled in his seat by the train window, Alec read *A Guide to Yokohama,* which Raymond, always concerned about the welfare of his younger brother, had placed in his coat pocket. Looking at the pictures, he remembered his father talking about his own visits to Yokohama, the largest Japanese harbor city of more than three million inhabitants. His father had also mentioned Commodore Perry, the American who had opened isolated Japan for foreign trade in 1854. Alec's city guide stated that by the end of the nineteenth century, Yokohama had become the most international city in Japan. "Surely, this development will be useful for the improvement of my English language skills," Alec mused.

Information about the great Kanto earthquake, which destroyed much of Yokohama in 1923, was less worrisome to Alec than learning that thirty American air-raids on the city during WWII had killed more than 8,000 people in one day. Only five years had passed since the war's end, and Alec was concerned that there might still be much destruction in the city. He hoped that the Americans, who now used the city as a shipping base, might have reconstructed most of it.

He read that the world's largest lighthouse would be visible from the train before it entered into the harbor, so he kept on the lookout for it. With some excitement, he also discovered that an immense Chinatown was located in the vicinity. He hoped this would not be too far from St. Joseph College. "I'm sure I'll miss my mother's Chinese steamed dumplings and barbecued riblets," he thought. Indeed, he was quite hungry right then on the train, but he would wait for the cheaper food available in Yokohama.

Shifting his attention from Chinese delicacies to his school prospectus, he read that St. Joseph College was founded in 1901 by the Catholic Marianist Society for "the education especially of foreign youths in Japan." The Marianist Fathers had already established a Japanese school and a commercial school in Nagasaki and Osaka. To Alec's delight, his school—really a combination of high school and college—looked out over the Yokohama harbor on one side and the International Cemetery on the other. He liked the multicultural orientation of his new environment. He learned that in 1943 the occupying Japanese army took over the campus for government purposes and the Marianist school evacuated to Hakone. The Marianists returned in 1945 when the Japanese (under American occupation) restored the college as an all-boys' school.

Now there were more than five hundred boys at St. Joseph, with teachers and students coming from all over the world. No narrow nationalism, Alec thought. With equal pleasure, he read about the school's strong soccer team, a sport that had become very popular in Japan. The prospectus noted, "Our international team was so good we had to play against college teams, and we still won the city championship. Word got around the globe, and sailors arriving in Yokohama eagerly anticipated soccer matches against us—high school kids! To even out the teams, teachers from St. Joseph joined in. And they were ferocious."

Upon arrival at St. Joseph, Alec felt immediately accepted by the registrar and the German headmaster Father Wilhelm. They inquired about Alec's studies in Hong Kong, his favorite subjects, and sports. They traced his parents' immigration and business ventures, and were angry about his cold-hearted treatment by the Japanese immigration authorities.

As in Hong Kong, Alec did not reside at the school. His living quarters had been arranged by his father whose friend, a Japanese businessman, offered housing in his home. Alec had just a corner of a room for sleeping and studying. From there he could observe much of the family life. Because his father's friend often returned home late at night, Alec spent many evenings talking to the man's wife, who offered him food and poured her heart out in regards to her husband's inconsiderate behavior. Like a typical Japanese businessman, the husband used to visit a tavern where he found friendship, entertainment, and comfort after work while his wife had to wait at home, available until late at night to serve his food, bath, and massage. There seemed to be little exchange of concern and emotion between them.

At school, Alec had to follow a prescribed curriculum, patterned after the British grammar schools. However, Alec was two years behind the level of other students in his class. Some subjects were taught in Japanese, but most were in English. Alec managed his studies well in both languages, though his English was still limited in vocabulary and syntax.

He kept up with the pace of his classes, but he excelled in sports—soccer above all. His photo collection from Yokohama shows a number of pictures with his soccer teams, including a match against the French Navy. Among those photos, a special place in his album is given to the game of Saint Joseph College against Misei on Oct. 25, 1952, in which SJC won the Japan National High School Championship. Even though he broke his leg during one of his games, Alec remained a highly appreciated player until the end of high school.

Toward the end of his first year at St. Joseph College, Alec began to feel uncomfortable in his rented corner of a room where he was too easily pulled into the landlady's confidence. After some searching for a new living arrangement, Alec found a job as house boy for an American military couple. Lieutenant Fred B. Holley and his wife, also a lieutenant, lived in the Yokohama harbor area, not far from his College. As a house boy,

French Navy vs. SJC, May 1952 (Alec, back row, on right).

St. Joseph College soccer team (Alec: back row, fourth from left).

Alec was expected to keep the house clean and to take care of the kitchen duties. His photo shows him smiling in front of the immaculate kitchen area. He was well treated, had a room of his own, could earn a small amount of money, and enjoyed some form of a family life.

Alec in the kitchen at the Holley home.

On the back of the photo, Alec wrote, "Lt. Fred B. Holley became a friend since July 1952." Naturally, this new housing arrangement was significant for him since English was the daily means of communication.

Just as in the businessman's home, where he observed a Japanese style of married life, Alec now gained insight into the daily life of an American couple. He noticed much more inter-action between husband and wife; they went out together or kept busy at home together. Tensions only developed occasion-ally. The wife kept "the upper hand" in regards to military issues, where her own military position was more advanced than that of her husband, and she made use of this advantage in no uncertain terms. Used to seeing Japanese women who obeyed their husbands, this was a new insight for Alec.

"I only observed, but I was not drawn into the disputes like in the Japanese family. This was a happy and safe time for me, and I learned a lot during my year as house boy. I gained a manner of insight into the western style of living and marriage. My English skills improved and I enjoyed the spontaneous conversations in which I often was encouraged to participate." Also, he had been able to save the modest amount of money he was paid for his services beyond his regular assignments. A year later the Holleys were recalled to a different part of the country and Alec was quite sad to lose his friends. The new army post offered to him was not as helpful, so he had to refuse the offer.

Alec (far right) stands next to Father Wilhelm, with some of his teammates.

CHAPTER 8

FRIEND AND PROTECTOR, FATHER WILHELM

Knowing that he would soon need new accommodations, Alec began searching for another place to live near his school. He soon found a cheap room with a Japanese widow and her two children, but in this new arrangement he had to pay his rent in cash. There was no exchange of services for rent nor the opportunity to earn additional income as before. He had to find a job.

While searching for employment, he realized that no Japanese businesses could hire him. Chinese nationals were not allowed to work in Japan. Alec assumed that the Japanese did not have the generosity to offer work or advantages toward their former enemies. Also Japan was overcrowded with immigrants who had fled the Communist regime in China.

He found employment in a Chinese laundry that, for low wages, disregarded the rules, but soon the night-time working hours interfered with his school assignments, and, worst of all, his body became overwhelmed with back pain. A Japanese bone specialist diagnosed him with progressive *Ankilosis Spondylitis,* a particularly severe type of arthritis, and warned him that healing this condition was rarely possible. The injections that Alec received in six-month intervals controlled the pain, but he felt physically weak, overwhelmed, and under-nourished, due to cheap and limited nutrition. This medical diagnosis reminded him that his maternal uncle had walked bent over at an almost ninety-degree angle. Alec wondered, "Do I have the same disease? Will my body become like that of my uncle in China?"

For income, he began selling paper and pencils from door to door, like a peddler, an experience that—combined with his weakening body—brought him to the end of his resistance, physical as well as mental. There were nasty rejections by householders, who dampened his self worth and robbed him of hope. When he collapsed at school and was taken to the infirmary, he had to explain his troubles to Father Wilhelm, the principal.

"Let me ponder what I can do," the Headmaster said in his heavy German accent. "My heart sang," Alec explained, "when the priest returned with the offer of working as his office boy in exchange for room and board at the college. I accepted without restraint, grateful to have my livelihood secured."

For the first time since leaving Taiwan, Alec felt like he belonged within the protective school community, with peers his own age. From then on, he did his best to satisfy Father Wilhelm, who let him know that he appreciated his efforts. "He even forgave me when I blew up his woodstove one winter, covering his books and papers with ashes and black soot," Alec recalled. Once again, he was treated with generosity and understanding.

Saint Joseph College remained Alec's home for the year and a half left until his graduation in 1955. Staying in the dorm led to closer friendships with other students for which he'd had hardly any time when he lived off campus. As in Hong Kong, he became a significant leader on his soccer team, a respected member of the group, and a generous helper whenever there was need. Alec also shared leisure activities that had not been accessible to him before. On a Sunday excursion he climbed Mount Fuji for the first time, realizing a long-held desire. A number of pictures show scenes of the ascending paths where he met two nurses who befriended him, shared their lunch, and later also invited him to their home. He often talked about this enjoyable encounter, and that he was treated with kindness and friendship.

Admiration for the city of Yokohama, its history, international spirit, and traditional and modern festivals, was mentioned often in Alec's stories about his years in this city and at his beloved St. Joseph College, where Father Wilhelm became like a second father to him.

Graduating from St. Joseph College, 1955.

The traditional silk letter of well-wishes from Alec's family.

CHAPTER 9

GRADUATION, INTERNMENT, UNEXPECTED WEALTH

In the spring of 1956, Alec sent home his high school graduation certificate. Like his brother Raymond two years earlier,
he graduated with high honors. Alec was proud to show him,
and his parents, an achievement based on his own initiative.

With similar pride and elation he also told his family that
he had been awarded a four-year scholarship to an American
college, DePaul University in Chicago. Much of this was
achieved with the help of his protector, Father Wilhelm, who
helped him secure the scholarship as well as a grant for room
and board. A sponsor in Washington, DC, committed the funds
for four years, as well as the travel money from Yokohama to
San Francisco.

Alec told his parents that he planned to study microeco-
nomics and business so that he would be able to help his father
reestablish his business after graduation. When his extended
family was informed of Alec's success in his studies and his
scholarship to study at an American University, they sent one
of the traditional "silk letters" of well-wishes to him. It held
the signatures of all of his family members in congratulations

for his success and their good wishes for his future. This common custom shows that the shame Alec had brought on the family some four years before had been forgiven.

* * *

Unfortunately for Alec, American scholarship regulations for foreign students required that he not enter the United States until August 1956. He would have to remain in Japan for six months after graduation because he did not have the extra money required to go home to Taipei. Since the annual registration as a foreigner in Japan was due in the spring, Alec planned this as his first task after graduation. He remembered the inflexibility of Japanese rules and their immediate enforcement.

Still full of joy and expectation, in view of his bright future, he went to the city office in Yokohama.

"Oh, you are no longer a student. Now that you have graduated, you no longer have reason for living in Japan," the official stated.

"But I'll leave Japan in six months. Here are my scholarship papers for studies in America," Alec answered.

"As a Chinese citizen you are not allowed to work while living here. You need to return to Taiwan immediately."

"I do not have the funds to return to Taiwan, only a visa to travel to the U.S. in six months."

"In that case," the official said, "I have to take you directly to the internment camp for aliens. Your friends will have to supply you with your daily needs."

Alec's mood fell quickly from elation to abject depression. "To whom could I turn for help? My parents were too far away to help me. My former landlady was too poor to help. I wondered whether I should explain to Father Wilhelm what happened. He was the one who knew me best and might be willing to vouch for me." It took a while until he was granted a telephone call by the camp supervisor. After the call, Father Wilhelm—highly agitated with the callous treatment given to one of his students by the Japanese officials—came at once to the camp. He gained immediate release for Alec with the commitment that he would be financially responsible for his Chinese student.

The faithful priest found him accommodations for a few days but St. Joseph College was closed for the summer months so Alec had to rent a room with a widow and her two children, using up the last of his finances. How could he earn his livelihood while waiting for departure in August? How could he earn the $600 required to prove to the American consulate that he would not enter the country as a dependent? He knew that the rising economy in Yokohama needed employees with strong English language skills. However, as before, a Chinese person with these skills would not be allowed to work by law.

Since his Japanese was fluent and without accent, Alec decided to simply adopt a Japanese name and introduce himself as a Japanese citizen when applying for a job. He asked his landlady if he might use her family name and she agreed. But then, not wanting to cause her trouble, Alec made up his own name, instead.

"My knowledge of English just might save me," Alec thought. He applied for a position with an international shipping company that required meeting and negotiating with the crews on incoming international tankers, freighters, and passenger liners for their throw-away items, such as leftover metal pieces, grain left in holding tanks, furniture, leftover food provisions, anything no longer of use. With three to four sailors, he would drive a boat out to an anchored ocean liner and ask permission to meet with the ship's purser. He would then identify and negotiate the purchase. For this work, a knowledgeable English negotiator was needed. "Will you be able to master this job, which also puts you in charge of the crew on our contact boat?" the shipping company officer asked him. The company offered a regular monthly payment, with additional percentages based on unusual purchases. Alec was more than happy with this offer and the fact that nobody suspected his background. In the bargain, he would also gain connections with the crew on an ocean liner that might, eventually, take him across the Pacific to America.

The introduction to rough sailors and rocky boats was done quickly. Since Alec didn't act like a fussy scholar and could take some rough jokes, he quickly blended in with the team. For the next five months, the crew operated the boat through the harbor and approached ships from Greece, Holland, Norway, and Spain. They found Greek ships the most hospitable while some Norwegians waved them away with contempt. Usually, after boarding permission was given, Alec and a helper investigated the objects offered for sale and negotiated the price with the ship's purser. Via telephone with his company, he could sign the contract and transport small loads home, or call for a bigger freight boat. He liked the challenge of negotiation and also the discovery of salable goods.

"On my luckiest trip," Alec liked to tell, "I noticed a heavy copper wire circling the hull of a Greek ship. Was this protection against sea mines still necessary, more than ten years after the war? I wondered, and asked the treasurer if the copper wire would be for sale. When his reply was positive, my company was elated. The Japanese electronics industry was in need of copper, a rare metal in Japan. As time went on, I discovered many ships with copper wire protection for which the treasurer gladly accepted money from our company. Everybody celebrated my good business sense and I gained one bonus after another. At the end of my work I was rich, even beyond the $600 that I needed to enter the United States."

Alec was happy with his work and well accepted among the sailors. Close to his departure to the United States, the company prepared a farewell party for him and slaughtered several chickens, still a delicacy in Japan after the war. On this occasion, he told his boss that he was Chinese and had introduced himself under a wrong name. "This fact did not matter to him," Alec explained, "because by now the company knew me for who I was, and what I could do, not for my nationality. This cordial leave-taking and friendly acceptance left very warm and happy memories in my mind and heart."

Another warm, but also embarrassing, memory of this time was more personal. The Japanese widow in whose home he had rented a room had become quite dependent on his help. Her twelve-year-old son liked Alec and they played soccer together whenever there was time. He also helped the boy with his school work. Over time, the boy's sister Helen indicated that she was fond of Alec and her mother hinted at a possible union in the future. Marriage arrangements at such a young age were still very common in Japan. Thinking of his plans to study in America, Alec could not encourage this dream. He hinted that he was a Christian and his church would not allow him to marry a Buddhist. He remained kind toward her, as to a sister, but hardly realized her determination when he took leave from Yokohama.

Helen, 1954.

CHAPTER 10

YOKOHAMA – SAN FRANCISCO – CHICAGO

After the farewell from the Yokohama shipping company, Alec took leave from Father Wilhelm with a mixture of sadness and joyful anticipation, keeping in his heart the spirit of this caring priest.

At the beginning of August, 1956, a group of Alec's friends, among them his landlady and her daughter, accompanied him to the pier where the freighter, *Old Colony Mariner,* was anchored, proudly displaying her multiple derricks and lifting equipment. The boat was a matter-of-fact freighter, not a pleasant luxury liner for tourists. It carried fewer than twenty passengers, among them several army men traveling home on furlough or dismissal from the military.

At the pier Alec was met by an American soldier, a friend of his former landlord, Lieutenant Fred Holley, who had asked Alec to take along a package for a family in Chicago. Alec was shocked to discover that it was a box containing a six-person set of china, fragile and heavy. Little did he realize that at the end of the journey this favor would cause him a great deal of trouble.

When the freighter left the harbor and reached the high seas, Alec did not feel so well. He explained, "My cabin was on the lowest deck, had no window, and, being close to the machine room, became intolerably hot. Having spent so much time in small rocky boats out on the ocean, I thought my body had overcome sea sickness, but sadly, I succumbed to the worst physical misery I had ever experienced. Neither the well-prepared food, nor the more stalwart passengers' concerns for me, nor the anticipation of the future firm ground in America soothed my sickness until on the fourth day my body adjusted to the freighter's rocking motion." Alec gradually enjoyed chatting with other passengers, joined their card games, and followed the captain's invitation, where he explained the machinery and important functions of the freighter. Alec and Joe, the returning soldier, often conversed on deck. He gave Alec insight into life in the U.S. military and his service in Japan, as well as a preview of what to expect in America.

The trip was never boring, and the sea breeze softened the hot sun during the day. The two-week voyage continued on calm seas. Close to San Francisco, Alec suggested to Joe that they share a hotel room once they arrived in the city. Joe agreed, but somewhat reluctantly. To Alec it seemed like a good idea, since both of them needed to limit expenses.

From the harbor, Alec followed the captain's suggestions for inexpensive hotels. By telephone, he inquired about a two-bed accommodation and found one immediately. Using public transportation to the hotel, Alec discovered that handling the box of china in addition to his own luggage was quite a burden.

On arrival at the hotel where he had reserved the room, the receptionist looked at Alec and asked, "Who is the second person?"When he pointed at Joe, the tall black-skinned soldier, the receptionist shook his head commenting, "There must have been a misunderstanding. We do not have any two-bed accommodation open at this moment." Alec started to argue that just a short time ago he had been assured of a double vacancy, while Joe quietly turned around and walked away. Joe knew what the comment meant, and Alec now understood his original reluctance. His first experience in America was that of the racial divisions in the country.

Instead of showing hurt or anger, Joe turned around and said, "Let me call my aunt living in San Francisco, maybe we can stay with her." And they did, with a cordial welcome and some joyful conversations.

Joe's relatives drove Alec to the Greyhound bus station the next day, where he bought a ticket for the three-day trip to Chicago. What a distance, Alec thought, compared to getting around the small islands of Japan and Taiwan.

When he stowed the Holleys' box of china in the Greyhound bus cargo compartment, he learned that he needed to pay an extra $64 for this transportation. He was confused and angry, but remembered Lieutenant Holley's promise that the receiving party would pay for all his expenses.

On the ride to Chicago, Alec took lively interest in the sights along the road. His photo album collection includes images of Nevada City, the expanse of Great Salt Lake, a church in Salt Lake City, and various scenes of flat or mountainous landscapes, ending with the impressive architecture of the Baha'i Temple in Wilmette, Illinois.

Members of the Catholic Student Union and their associated parents, volunteering to receive foreign students, helped settle Alec in his dormitory in DePaul University, and then acquainted him with the city. He always mentioned how accommodating and caring people were when he reached his final stop in Chicago.

Having lived in large cities in both China and Japan, Alec was able to adjust quickly. He felt relieved to leave behind Japanese society, where Chinese were considered lower class citizens. His work experience with the American Army personnel in Yokohama had taught him that Americans would be far more tolerant of Chinese citizens than the Japanese.

However, delivery of the gift box from Yokohama to a distant Chicago suburb reminded Alec that people could not always be trusted. The family, in the middle of a big party, kept him at the entrance door like a servant and simply handed him a check to cover his costs. Then the check was rejected at the bank for lack of funds! On a second trip to see the owner to whom he'd delivered the gift, Alec finally received the money in a matter-of-fact transaction without apology.

Alec returned to campus, bitterly disappointed by this deception and the uncaring encounter with the family. Transporting a box with heavy china along with his own luggage had been a demanding task. Trustworthy friends advised him to be more cautious in selecting people to whom he offered this kind of generous help.

CHAPTER 11

LIFE AS A COLLEGE STUDENT IN CHICAGO

Alec moved into the Kolping House, a German hostel where Father Wilhelm had secured his lodging for the duration of his studies. He found well-ordered surroundings, but not always friendly acceptance from some of the German journeymen who kept aloof from foreigners or made denigrating remarks. On the contrary, Jim Fritts, an American engineering student also living at Kolping House, appreciated Alec's experiences and his philosophizing nature. They often exchanged views about life and their studies, becoming fast friends.

Alec with Jim Fritts at DePaul.

Alec was doing well in courses that were not intensively language related, but experienced difficulties when papers were due. His writing skills functioned far below his verbal skills. He often had to hire an English language expert to read and correct his written work. Jim also helped with his papers for English composition classes. Alec's English Composition instructor was very discouraging and critical of his written English. She threatened not to pass him. He earned high marks, however, in all of his other classes, and felt very proud when he could inform Father Wilhelm that he was living up to his expectations.

He maintained his relationship to the Catholic Student community, expanding his insight into his adopted Christian faith. Along with Jim, Alec joined the Student Smokers' Club where, over discussions of economics, the participants smoked cigarettes or pipes. He preferred a pipe since it was "so very British." He also found companionship in meetings with foreign students at DePaul.

Alec discovered an abiding interest in questions that concerned the meaning of life. In some of his classes, he strongly responded to problems of philosophical nature and yearned for deeper understanding. By taking a number of courses in philosophy—which were not required for his degree in economics—he began to gain more insight into this field of study that explores fundamental ideas about knowledge, nature, truth, values, and the meaning of life. It is no wonder that the experiences in Alec's early years led him to search for answers to these vital questions.

As was his habit, Alec sent detailed letters to his parents and brother, while news from them returned regularly. Their welfare worried him. His father had been able to rebuild his business and repay some of his debt, but Alec remained concerned that some of his risky business activities might not be legal under the Chiang Kai-shek government. But what could he understand or advise from a different continent?

Alec's study grant provided him with a monthly small allowance that occasionally he was able to supplement with jobs that he found with help of the Student Employment Office. He had enough to live on, but not enough to help his family.

When Alec met a fellow DePaul student, Fred, who had also attended St. Joseph College in Yokohama, he was introduced to the Hiakawas, a Japanese family in Chicago, where he could find sanctuary at any time. Mr. Hiakawa was retired, and owned a bass boat at Crystal Lake. Fred was his nephew, and together they introduced Alec to fishing, which he promptly adopted as his most relaxing hobby. They continued their acquaintance over occasional picnics and fishing trips. Mrs. Hiakawa always impressed visitors with her gentle service and warmhearted interest. Through the Hiakawas, Alec experienced a more loving Japanese family life than he had observed in Japan. Both Mr. and Mrs. Hiakawa had spent four years in American concentration camps for the Japanese during World War II, but they never showed any bitterness about this deprivation of freedom in their outward expressions. Mrs. Hiakawa talked about workshops the prisoners developed. She showed Alec her pieces of jewelry made of little sea shells and rocks.

Alec looked healthy and husky on his fishing trips with the Hiakawas. When he sent pictures home to Taiwan, his family assumed he was well to do and now able to send more support, but to maintain his own monthly obligations he worked more hours than ever. Also these images of radiant health were deceiving. His arthritis, which had plagued him with persistent pain in Japan, continued to bother him daily in his new environment. A physician in the Student Health System offered the same diagnosis and prescribed pain medication, which from then on gave him the bodily strength needed to keep up with his studies with only occasional painful interruptions.

An ear operation during these undergraduate years also became very troublesome. When Alec insisted on a checkup some time later, no physician wanted to treat him. The operation had been done by an intern who had since left the hospital, and it seemed nobody remembered his name. On Alec's insistence the hospital assigned a new physician, who discovered a piece of gauze had been left inside the ear canal causing painful inflammation. Alec did not have the means or necessary information to find legal support at the time.

At DePaul, Alec also enjoyed companionship with female students. In his second year, he developed strong feelings for a woman who had helped him with his English. Alec liked her outgoing personality. In her picture, she appears vivacious and attractive. When he consulted his parents regarding a possible marriage, they refused permission because of her Jewish background. I believe she was quite attached to Alec, but he never told her why he did not allow their relationship to develop deeper roots.

While Alec was busy studying in Chicago, Raymond completed the required military service in Taiwan and proudly sent Alec a photo of himself in uniform.

Now that he had been discharged from the military and was ready to get married, Raymond learned about the marriage contracts their parents had arranged when both he and Alec were children. Raymond's match would have been of great advantage for their father's fragile business, but his affection belonged to a different woman: Masako. When Raymond finally confessed that he would be marrying Masako instead, he was released from his contractual obligation but the young woman, her parents, and his own parents were bitterly disappointed. Why had he revealed this only a day before his wedding to Masako?

Raymond and Masako married, and sent Alec a photograph so he could share the occasion for which he had sent $500, his entire monthly stipend plus additional money from temporary jobs.

Masako and Raymond, 1959.

Masako and Raymond's wedding photograph, 1959.

In early 1960, in the months just prior to Alec's graduation, a letter from his family carried a shocking message. His father wrote, "We have undergone a second bankruptcy, this time without hope for recovery. We are reduced to basic living, yet do not worry. We are able to live modestly with Raymond's and Masako's help." The enclosed pictures showed Alec's father on his bicycle, ready to take off on his daily trips peddling trinkets and other wares. A second photo showed Raymond ironing clothes in a Chinese laundry, even with his distinguished degree and high achievement in English! Finally, there was a photograph of his mother next to Masako, working at the same laundry: one folding garments and the other on the sewing machine.

At the conclusion of the letter, Alec's father made a statement significant for Alec's future. "With this second business failure, you are released from any obligation to the family business, which is now nonexistent. We no longer need your business expertise. For your graduate studies, choose a field of your own interest and I will be happy with your decision."

Alec had become especially interested in philosophy during his undergraduate studies, and this newfound freedom from family obligation opened up new possibilities. However, his worry over his family's economic balancing act had increased significantly.

Another family issue yet to be resolved was the question of Alec's marriage contract. His intended bride was the second daughter of the same family that had been disappointed by Raymond. Alec felt he could not marry a woman he did not know. Since he could not travel back to Taiwan, Alec suggested she come and live in the U.S. for a while to test compatibility between them. Naturally her family would not allow their daughter to risk her innocence by going to a foreign country without family protection so the marriage contract was dissolved, leaving Alec free to find his own partner in marriage.

He was not without choices. Via letter, he learned that the daughter of his former landlady in Japan had converted to Catholicism and been baptized in hopes this might lead to marriage. Alec was surprised and felt somewhat guilty. He was still a student and not ready to have a visitor from abroad, much less to think of marriage. What could he do to satisfy her expectations? As with the arranged marriage, Alec suggested the girl spend a stretch of time in Chicago first, which she and her mother refused.

Helen

CHAPTER 12

FROM GRADUATION TO GRADUATE STUDENT

Alec's graduation from DePaul University was hardly a festive event for him without members of his family present, but seeing the Hiakawas among the crowd of congratulants lifted his spirit. They threw a party for him after the ceremony, and there Alec explained that he had been accepted for graduate studies in philosophy at Loyola University. First he needed to catch up with some undergraduate courses in this new field, and then he would receive a substantial scholarship.

"No wonder he'll study philosophy. He has been puzzling about the meaning of life while challenged by so many big decisions in his youth," Mister Hiakawa said. "It is my reading of Dostoevsky's novels that initiated my fascination with philosophical reflections," Alec explained.

Father Hecht S.J., his advisor and department head at Loyola University, also seemed to recognize Alec's questioning mind. Like Father Wilhelm in Yokohama, Father Hecht became his academic advisor, personal guide, and friend in Chicago throughout his graduate studies and in the years to follow.

Alec's photo album ends with a graduation picture from DePaul University, followed by a second photo of himself with the words, "The First Day of my New Life."

After Alec completed his undergraduate studies, his allotted time in the Kolping House was over. He found accommodation in the apartment of a bachelor pastry chef who created artistic pastries for the German Bismarck restaurant downtown. Alec's roommate was pleased he had found a companion who appreciated German order and neatness, while Alec was grateful to share his ideas and interests with a lively, down-to-earth companion. This fellow was also a creative cook at home, and Alec occasionally prepared Chinese-style dinners to share. It seemed that Alec was drawn toward people and things of German nature, all stemming from his close friendship with Father Wilhelm, the German headmaster of St. Joseph College back in Yokohama.

Toward the end of his undergraduate years and early graduate studies, Alec began visiting the Crossroads Student Center on the south side of the city, near the University of Chicago. The Crossroads Student Center was a meeting place for foreign students from a variety of local universities. Many college and graduate students came to the center, which was focused on building companionship and sharing general information about the area. There, Alec met with other students of various nationalities, faiths, and values, which he began to study along with his own.

He also began working weekends for the Santa Fe Railroad accounting office. They offered flexible schedules and appreciated his quick, reliable work style. His English language skills improved as he was exposed to idiomatic expressions in the office, and which often got him tangled in misunderstandings over the phone. "No soap" did not mean the absence of soap, but that something could not be done. "For crying out loud" did not mean he was crying out on the telephone but that someone was upset about his slow understanding. He also marveled at how one could "pour out the baby with the bath water" when you did not even have a baby? On the other end of the line, amusement or impatience were often the result.

Worries about his parent's economic struggles continued to weigh heavily on his mind throughout his graduate studies. There was no direct request for support, but the fact that his father and brother had to struggle hard to fulfill the monthly repayment of debts troubled him.

A visit from an uncle, his mother's brother, who held a high position in the Taiwanese government, did not relieve his worries. The uncle had come to enjoy himself in Chicago, going out to nightclubs, and sightseeing, using Alec as a chauffeur. His uncle did not understand that he was a student who had to count every penny. He also did not show much concern for Alec's family; after all, the man's sister, Alec's mother, now belonged to a different family clan. Alec often talked about him and his visit with much anger in his voice.

Alec confided with Father Hecht at Loyola about his family needs and obligations. He also sought advice from Father Fu, a Chinese priest, who ran a Catholic Student Center in downtown Chicago. After these conversations, Alec was sure of one task: he had to do his best in his studies. So, in spite of health and family troubles, his course work was always successful.

CHAPTER 13

STEPS TOWARD A FRIENDSHIP

My acquaintance with Alec began at the Crossroads Student Center. I was a visiting teacher from Germany. Crossroads was just a block away from my apartment, so I often stopped in to spend time with friends after a day's teaching at Loretta Academy High School.

I lived on the eleventh floor of a modern building named Indian Village, and my apartment became a gathering place for friends and staff I had met at Crossroads. They admired the wall of windows with a view of the lake, and the indoor garden laid out on the black linoleum floor with bricks that enclosed white pebbles from the lake and pots with flowers. In winter, the garden enclosed a Christmas tree.

My bi-weekly French group would gather around the rattan table, chatting and feasting on Burgundy, bread, and cheese. Foreign student friends came to share homeland memories and to cook some of their native dishes for all of us. There was Giovanni from Italy; Anna from Germany; Janesh from Israel; Rosita from the Philippines; Ernest from India; Denise from France; and Alec from China, among many others.

Eventually, Alec and I volunteered to help students gather in small national groups so they could find friends of their own national background. This plan called for many socials with the Crossroads administrative staff: Denyse, Simone, Hildegard, and Nadine, along with student organizers.

At meetings with larger groups, Alec was usually very quiet and withdrawn, sometimes hiding behind a game of chess. If challenged, he became lively and outgoing when he felt healthy and at ease.

Alec had many health problems at that time, which affected his vocal chords and hearing. When he had an operation at the University of Chicago Hospital, his Foreign Student Club friends visited him, including me. It was at this time that I learned about his family in Taipei, and his difficult and lonely childhood tossed from China to Hong Kong to Yokohama finally resulting in the young man who arrived in Chicago. Alec seemed very pleased and grateful to be remembered by his friends, but what we, as well as his family back in Taiwan, did not know was his additional near-constant pain from spinal inflammation and the heavy pain killers he was forced to take.

After I visited him in the hospital, Alec became more outgoing and self-revealing. I had pulled him away from the chessboard, where he liked to escape from the crowd. We started meeting up after lectures at Loyola, and even shared a seminar occasionally.

After he became secretary of the Inter-University Foreign Student Club, Alec visited the Crossroads Student Center more frequently. He decided a used car would make the commute less complicated than the use of the I.C. (Illinois Central Railroad) so he studied driving manuals, obtained his learner's permit, and got a few lessons from friends. At night, he drove the car through his neighborhood to gain skills and self confidence. Did he have too much of the latter when he failed the first driving test? After he did not pass the second test either, he became concerned. "I do not think I really make so many mistakes. What should I do to get the license?" he asked a friend. "Present a few dollar bills to the examiner. I am sure that will help," this friend suggested. And help it did. He passed on the third attempt.

Whether he always followed the traffic rules he had memorized for his learner's permit was another issue. I remember Alec pulling a U-turn on the six-lane Lake Shore Drive so as not to be late for the movie Oedipus Rex at the International Theater. He had invited me to see the movie, and I sure clung to my seat at this daring U-turn. Unfortunately, the traffic police stopped him and wrote a heavy fine on a pink piece of paper. Later, at the movie, King Oedipus' masked face seemed to mimic the same threatening expression that Alec had encountered from the "guardian of the roads."

After he bought the car, Alec was surprised and upset when he discovered that a considerable amount of money was deducted from his paycheck. "This is wage assignment for your car insurance," his employer explained. When giving his signature at the time of purchase, Alec had not been informed that the money for car insurance would be collected in that manner. Mr. Hiakawa's son, a lawyer, explained, "Insurance agents use the ignorance of immigrants this way. For them it is the easiest way to collect their fees." He then saw to it that Alec's agreement was changed to personal payments.

Now with a car and a driver's license, Alec invited his friends for rides to the nearby Museum of Science and Industry. He and I went several times and often had a picnic on the museum grounds afterward. My Jewish friends, Barbara and Bernie Baum, joined us at times or offered their own picnic. We enjoyed Alec's company and his vivid descriptions of the life he had left behind.

Alec befriended a philosophy student from Germany and the three of us would go to the movies or attend a lecture followed by discussions. One of our favorite luxuries led us to the harbor area. In a small shack, fresh shrimp directly from the boat were fried and offered for immediate sizzling consumption in the car. The Santa Fe Railroad office was in the neighborhood, and Alec's colleagues had introduced him to this treat that reminded him of the fresh seafood in Yokohama.

When our friend returned to Germany, Alec and I continued our occasional small trips: to the Brookfield Zoo, the arboretum, and the Baha'i Temple in Wilmette.

During the summer, he invited me for a trip to the Wisconsin Dells that was so often mentioned as a place of natural beauty and magical entertainment. This was our first trip to Wisconsin. In the Dells, we enjoyed our first pow-wow, which was powerful and exciting. On a boat ride along the Wisconsin River, which snaked through the deep cuts of the sandstone bed, we grasped the significance of this geological structure that formed the Dells. We visited the military fort that introduced us to the cigar-smoking cowboy statue, patient enough to tolerate our many photos. During a picnic lunch at the Deer Park, we learned that the animals were smart enough to lead us to the feeding automat and lift the flap on the feeding machines.

That afternoon, Alec suffered from a severe case of hay fever. On the trip home he was desperate with fatigue and a headache, and asked me to drive.

"DRIVE?" I had a learner's permit only and no driving experience on the highway. I considered his pleading and reluctantly slid into the driver's seat, hoping to get directions and support from Alec, who was asleep by the time I had settled at the wheel. Like a robot fused to the wheel, I guided the car through the light traffic. When we reached the multi-forked, high-speed city highways, Alec was alert again and able to get behind the wheel.

On one of these trips to Wisconsin we went to Crystal Lake, where I was introduced to Alec's love of fishing. Mr. Hiakawa's bass boat seated four and left room enough for Alec and him to teach me to thread a worm, which I managed with only slight shudders of disgust. Yet my discomfort was quickly forgotten when my first cast brought up a painted turtle larger than my hand. I felt great pride holding the beautiful reptile with an orange and yellow design on her shell. That was to become the most interesting catch I ever made, far beyond the ordinary bluegills and sunfish. I noticed that Alec became expansive and fully relaxed when he could sit and wait for the surface movement on the water that indicated the presence of fish on the hook.

Visits to Brookfield Zoo, the botanical gardens, and to the many museums in the city further forged our friendship, but also showed me the high level of consideration Alec gave to friends, and his commitment to his work and studies. His free-flowing stories about his past formed an ever clearer picture in my mind. I was, and still am, a good listener, who admired and appreciated him.

Alec with his car.

CHAPTER 14

A TRUE FISH STORY

Among all of the foreign students who visited my apartment, Alec was the one who most enjoyed cooking. Noting the tiny cutting board in my apartment, he came over one day with a cutting board large enough to accommodate all of the mixed vegetable cuttings for his dishes. With some circumspection, I wondered about the big crab he also brought and cleaned off on the large cutting board.

While he worked, he told stories about Chinese delicacies, which some of us found difficult to appreciate. He reminisced about a big pot with live fishlets swimming in cool water, surrounding a large chunk of tofu in the center. While the water heated up to the boiling point, the fish penetrated the cooler soft tofu and ended up being cooked inside it. The paste was consumed with soy sauce and spices as a delicacy. I remember asking him to stick to dishes more palatable to western tongues, which he did gladly, often focusing on fish. He was greatly admired when he cooked from memory the Chinese dishes that he had seen his Mother prepare. He loved to cook for his friends. Over time he expanded his skills and prepared extensive meals.

On another occasion, Alec told me about the delicious Chinese carp and how to prepare it with vegetables. "You have so often mentioned inviting your lonely Aunt Sophie to dinner," he said. "Would you like for me to prepare a Chinese carp dinner for her?" Indeed, I had told him about my German aunt, a widow, who, after forty years in the States, had not yet mastered the English language. She had sold her elegant mansion and dwelled in a large apartment piled with oriental rugs, knickknacks, delicate porcelain, and silk upholstered furniture acquired on auction from wealthy Chicago homes. Now living alone, she felt isolated and dejected. With Alec's encouragement, I arranged the dinner date with her and a fellow teacher from my school who offered to drive her.

I do not remember the look on Aunt Sophie's face when the elevator brought her to the eleventh floor and she stepped into my apartment with its second-hand Asian furniture, brick-and-pebble garden, self-built book shelves, and a well-used recliner. My cotton dress did not match Sophie's elegant silky attire either, but I was in the kitchen helping Alec prepare the big fish he had caught in Wisconsin.

He removed the scales and made long cuts crisscrossing the body. He packed the openings high with vegetables to let the juice penetrate the fish body before it vanished into the oven to be baked. This allowed time to cook the rice and set the seaweed cracker hors d'oeuvres on the table with a glass of wine.

I had a premonition that Dick, my colleague, and a very traditional eater, might not like fish, and that Aunt Sophie might hold a certain prejudice against a Chinese cook preparing native dishes. But, so what, I thought, let them experience some more exotic dishes. Besides, I hoped that with a glass of wine the visitors' taste buds might become a bit blunted toward the new eating experience. Dick, in his usual gentlemanly style, directed the conversation to Aunt Sophie who, in broken English explained her indecision about returning to Germany, where she still had a brother living. It was not so much the trip she feared but the transport of the massive possessions that she thought she needed as a foundation for a new life in her home country.

During the conversation, I wondered whether she noticed the absence of curtains, carpets, ebony furniture, and exquisitely crafted Swedish and German porcelain in my apartment, that, to her mind, were so necessary for everyday life.

When the moment came to carry in the dishes, Fried Wonton was offered first, crisp and tasty, filled with ground pork, dipped in soy or sweet-sour sauce. A platter with rice followed, then mixed veggies with mushrooms and squid. Finally, Alec brought in the masterpiece: fish with attached head, open eyes, fins, and full tail. Chicken soup was announced as the final dish. According to Alec, four dishes were the minimal requirement for a Chinese dinner. All along, I had not wanted to squelch Alec's enthusiasm for offering Chinese dishes to my guests, but I worried that they might not be prepared for a meal of unfamiliar foods. So I was delighted when the wontons produced ahs and ohs: "as tasty as German fritters, even without the exotic sauce!" "The rice," I explained, "is a parallel to the German potatoes, please, make it the foundation for the veggies and the fish."

Both Dick and Aunt Sophie carefully pulled out the vegetables in between the squid slices which were fully equipped with arms and suction cups. I remember their leathery qualities when left on the edge of the plate. Meanwhile, everybody took parts of the fish's middle section with its crunchy skin and veggie-filled slits. Head and tail were carefully avoided. For all the outward beauty of the fish, its white flesh reminded one neither of trout nor of delicious walleye. It tasted plain muddy, and a second forkful was tried with great hesitation. Alec almost turned purple with embarrassment, commenting, "In China a carp is a highly desired fish because of his exquisite taste. I do not know what went wrong. He did look like a Chinese carp when I caught him."

Dick—an expert in English literature but inexperienced with hook and line—was able to clarify the problem. "Carp in American waters are mud eaters. They feed on the river bottom. In Japan I have seen that carp are raised in clear water when used for eating. Alec, you could not know that fishermen here do not even throw a carp back into the river because we do not want it among the other fish. Maybe see if your neighbor's cat is less sensitive to this 'mud puppy'."

All of us laughed off Alec's error and somehow found enough to eat, especially with the German buttercream torte from a fancy bakery for dessert. Alec realized that he had to become more cautious in the choice of dishes he offered to guests. He would shift his fishing to walleye, bass, and pan fish, and on special occasions to salmon and lake trout.

Aunt Sophie did not show much reaction to the dinner, for she greatly enjoyed being pulled out of her lonely life by an audience who politely and patiently listened to her. But I learned her true reaction several months later when I visited my parents in Germany. She had sent my parents a letter saying that I was living in rather primitive conditions. She had written that I was not wearing my usual jewelry. My simple cotton dress was an indication that I just was not well off. Most likely, I had sold the jewelry or pawned it to have enough money. She did not mention the failed dinner, but had hinted that I had some very unusual friends. All of these comments had my parents extremely worried about my welfare and lifestyle.

CHAPTER 15

REACHING OUT AND GATHERING IN

With the beginning of fall, 1962, I received invitations to the opera from Alec. One very special event was the Bolshoi Ballet's performance of *Swan Lake* at the city Opera House. The tickets were expensive, but with overtime work at Santa Fe, Alec was able to buy tickets. He would get so excited and joyful when he offered these special surprises. Sometimes they came in form of a large cutting board or a live crab from the Chinese food store, or a special dish he brought for a meal. I appreciated these unusual, thoughtful selections, which were sometimes accompanied by a beautiful poem with lines of admiration and gratitude.

"I think Alec's intentions are becoming more serious than friendship," said my friend Barbara Baum on one of our frequent visits. With just a gesture of my hand, I waved away the thought. We were students and just curious about other cultures; we liked to learn from each other. Soon, however, the idea would return.

Mr. Graham, the principal of Latin School where I was teaching, asked me to attend a three-day convention in Colorado Springs called "Religion in Secular Private Schools." I was chosen because I had organized the Monday morning

"Period of Reflection" during the previous year. Naturally, I accepted the offer with enthusiasm. I was given airline tickets and accommodations at the luxurious Broadmoor Hotel, where the convention was held.

Alec was nervously excited about the trip — even more than I — and offered to drive me to the airport. He was so excited that he overlooked a street sign and drove the wrong way onto a one-way street, right in the center of the city. He was immediately stopped by the city police and handed an expensive ticket. Being just a poor student this must have been a financial blow for him, but he did not want me to share the cost. After arranging to meet me after the return flight, I gave myself over to the joyful excitement of traveling. I was delighted to see a larger part of the U.S. from the air. The breathtaking mountains reminded me of the Austrian Alps.

The lectures were informative for my planning at Latin School, but in the evenings I found myself reclining on the king-sized bed pondering "the Alec Chiu relationship" and its future. A marriage proposal would bind me to the U.S. forever, or even possibly to Taiwan. My parents would be sad if I did not return to Germany.

Did our different cultural backgrounds matter to me? I pondered. Was our relationship not just emotional, but strongly built on shared religious and economic values? Were we able to listen to each other? How strongly would both parental families influence us? Lastly, what would our nine-year age difference mean for us? (I being the elder.) Would children be important to both of us?

I admired how Alec had overcome the deprivations of his past, and his generosity—toward friends, and especially to me. Above all, I appreciated his questioning attitude toward life and his search—not so much for success and money but for a life based on profound values. He had been a member of the Catholic Church since his time in Hong Kong.

Now, I remembered Barbara's words and understood that she had been more aware of the development of our emotional attachment than I had. I wondered how I should respond if Alec asked the important question. I returned to Chicago in anticipation of big decisions and with a restless but joyful mind.

CHAPTER 16

AN INTER-CULTURAL WEDDING

On my return from Colorado, Alec came up with the suggestion to "remain in the spirit" and attend the Birth of Buddha
Festival in Wilmette at the University of Chicago campus
there. The experience of being immersed in silence, inter-
rupted by occasional intonations of "OM," left a deep impression with us.

That fall, I celebrated the completion of my Master's degree
in Education from Loyola. None of my family members could
be present at the formal presentation of degrees, but as I
walked across the stage to receive my diploma I saw members
of the Baum family waving. Right then, I felt a very deep joy,
almost with tears in my eyes, realizing that the need for sharing
joy in life surpassed even the need for sharing sadness. As an
only child, I have always searched out companionship and
camaraderie. Being human means to live in community. The
presence of these special friends anchored my achievement.

Later, when celebrating over a special dinner, some friends
joked with Alec, "We hope that your next big non-academic
step will soon follow." They did not specify the step, but I knew
what they meant. I thought it would take a long time, but not

so. They were surprised when Alec and I announced our engagement only six weeks later.

Our relationship had been growing over years. At the beginning, we saw one another at Crossroads almost weekly. As time grew, our running conversations never found an end. Both of us considered our possible future plans. Alec's plans were dim and insecure, and I wavered between staying in the U.S. and returning to Germany. But we were both immigrants, and we both struggled to understand and integrate into American culture and society. He told me how Chinese family life was based on a mixture of traditional and business guidelines. The firm paternal family structure was new to me, in comparison to European and American family relationships. Alec struggled with how these might translate into American culture. Yet, he always felt that his own family connections had been superficial and very impersonal, following a very unusual pattern of living in separation.

On Thanksgiving, 1962, he proposed "a life together" and we were engaged. We had resolved the important question of our age difference. Alec considered it unimportant, except for the need to plan for a baby early into the marriage.

While Alec and I took steps toward our marital union, his parents in Taiwan planned to emigrate to Sao Paolo, Brazil. They hoped to begin a new livelihood there which was impossible in Taiwan due to their debts from previous business problems. Their plan to emigrate became a reality when Raymond agreed to shoulder his father's bankruptcy debts so that his parents could leave the country. Alec followed Raymond's new obligations with much concern, after all Raymond had two young sons to support as well. He fondly remembered his brother's support and care during his own elementary school and early teen years, when their parents were busy or traveling. Now, Alec did not like to see Raymond burdened with parental debt, nor did we feel prepared to take on their old—and new—obligations.

Why we set the wedding date for only two months later, on January 23, 1963, I do not remember. It was at the beginning of a school semester for me and Alec was writing his final thesis for his Masters in Philosophy. Perhaps his parents thought it would be a time of good omen. They certainly were delighted about our engagement. My own parents were accepting but sad since they had hoped I would return to Germany to live. My friends at the Crossroads Student Center, at the Baum household, and at my Chicago Latin school, everyone who knew and appreciated Alec and me, were joyous and helpful with preparations. We envisioned a modest wedding ceremony only, with close friends, nothing showy that needed intricate preparations.

I had hoped we could take our vows at the small chapel at Crossroads, where several other interracial weddings of our friends had been performed. For many foreign students, this Center had become a home abroad. However, the new priest at my parish church refused permission. He asked us to have the ceremony in the big, impersonal St. Thomas church where I had been a parishioner but only an occasional visitor at times when the student center had no priest available. Even my tears could not shake his resolve. The parish priest explained, "If unions fall apart in the future, the question will be, who has given permission for a wedding ceremony outside the parish?" Unable to change his mind, we called my uncle, Rev. Joseph Blank, S.J. at St. Louis University, who gladly agreed to come and bless our marriage vows at St. Thomas church.

The Crossroads community offered to host the reception. Fellow teachers from the Latin School, Ellie Lambrakis and Richard Dolezal, would "stand up" for us. Ellie offered to design and sew my dress. She and I went to Mandel's Department Store basement sales to look for dress material and found beautiful white cotton damask, and a short veil to match. She made the most beautiful calf-length dress, with long sleeves and a boat neck-line for my wedding. The overall cost for the outfit was eleven dollars. This simple ceremony was a celebration within our means and in close connection with our friends and family.

On the night before the wedding, I stayed at the Crossroads where my friends and I chatted and dispersed any anxiety. Yet, when alone in my bedroom, I struggled as I had so often in the preceding weeks with the question of where this significant step in my life would lead me. Would we be able to build a peaceful family? Yet above these reflections, I had no doubt that I would have a reliable and caring partner. My only sad thoughts were for my parents who now would give up their hope for my return to Germany. It hurt, to take away their expectation.

The wedding day itself was cold, gray, and rainy. My uncle (the priest) had reminded me to be on time, saying that he had once walked out on a couple who were unacceptably late. Why this gloomy comment? We came from a family that liked order and punctuality!

Trudging through wet muddy snow, Alec and I, followed by our guests, reached the small side chapel decorated with white daisies. A bunch of daisies in my arm, Alec and I walked to the altar and celebrated Mass with our friends. While each prayed in their own way, we felt their joy and love when we said our marriage vows. We were a multi-cultural, multi-religious crowd of Catholics, Lutherans, Buddhists, and Jews, from the U.S., Germany, Greece, Japan, France, and Holland. We had invited twenty-five guests; among them were Father Joseph Blank, S.J., my father's brother and the priest who would be the celebrant. Our four Crossroads friends, Denise, Simone, Nadine, and Anna were there. From Latin School came Ellie Lambrakis and Dick Dolezal. Five members of the Baum family shared the joy. Alec's friends, Mr. Hiakawa and his wife and son fit well into the group. For me, the closest relative was my cousin, Hans Theo Martin and his wife Sonna. Alec and I walked together down the aisle and were received by my uncle whose words of advice I have not remembered, but our vows we both kept and took seriously.

After the ceremony, friends assembled in the Crossroads Center's large living room. The table was set with shrimp salad, fruit and egg salads to accompany the sliced roast beef, crescent rolls and European "petit pains." Champagne, and white and red wines were on hand for toasting. All followed by an elaborately decorated buttercream torte from the German Konditorei bakery on Rush Street that Alec and I had frequently visited. This was no American-style, multi-level, tower-like cake, but rather a miracle of baking perfection in the horizontal.

Alec and Ursula.

We sat together and chatted after the meal, with the usual warm humor coming from friends to whom we owed so much gratitude and affection. Many cordial and humorous congratulations were offered, as well as memories of our shared activities.

After several hours of celebration, Uncle Joseph had to catch his train back to St. Louis so we drove him to the station. Before entering his compartment from the platform, he shook Alec's hand and said, "Welcome into the Blank Family. We are glad to have you."

I replied, "I am so proud that a member of the Blank family could administer our wedding vows." Then Uncle Joseph entered the train and left, an old man, for whose loneliness I felt sorry, and whose gruffness I could not easily accept. Yet, I knew he was dedicated to the family and to our well-being.

Ellie with the bride.

Denise and Simone with the happy couple.

Reception at the Crossroads Center.

CHAPTER 17

GROWING INTO MARRIED LIFE

My large efficiency apartment on the eleventh floor at Indian Village became our first abode. The ten large windows made it a sunny and roomy place. Looking out from the wall of windows, we appreciated Lake Michigan's changing moods and the scraps of clouds sailing between the other twelve-story buildings. The apartment complex was like an island within the fast-changing neighborhood on Chicago's South Side.

In the living room, we expanded our bookshelves with boards and bricks to hold our combined library. Second-hand Indonesian rattan furniture offered pleasant visiting and dining areas that also included a comfortable recliner. The couch on the other wall of the large room converted into a double bed, a generous donation from our friends the Baums. Alec extended a storage space in front of the bathroom with a large armoire, which now held our shared possessions. Fortunately, the kitchen was wide enough to allow two cooks at a time. We were satisfied and very proud of our creative and unusual living/studying space.

Alec continued to work three-day-weekend shifts at the Santa Fe Railroad office. I was busy preparing daily classes and checking student papers for my teaching at Latin School.

On weekends we visited the Baums, who lived just three blocks away.

Because of my advanced age, Alec and I planned for a baby from the beginning. We were happy and surprised when I realized that I was pregnant in April. We gathered advice about jobs and baby planning. I worried about how we could create financial security and a healthy environment for our child to come.

My teaching position at Latin School was secure. Alec was secure at Santa Fe Railroad. He also spent time finishing the foreign language requirement for his M.A. in Philosophy. He had hoped that his fluency in Japanese would count, but instead he needed to pass the test in French which was a big disappointment.

Our modest weekend outings included visits to the shrimp shacks along the harbor. In late spring fishermen pulled from the lake nets of silvery smelt that we could buy and fry at home. We also visited the International Movie House on Michigan Avenue and the Art Institute. We carefully controlled our finances. Money was important for raising a baby. Would there be enough?

Both of us were shocked when post-wedding congratulations arrived from Brazil: "We are so happy you are married. Now work together to help get your parents on their feet again. Together, you must at least earn $20,000 a year and will be able to do so. Help us to settle in our new business so that eventually we can spend our retirement years in the United States."

"I do not owe any support to my parents," Alec had promised me before our marriage. "As a second son, father has declared me free of obligation to the family, according to Confucian law." Why did we now receive requests from them for various needs?

This was my first contact with my parents-in-law! How could we meet these expectations with only a small amount of savings in the bank? Soon after this letter we were asked to repay a Japanese businessman from whom his parents had borrowed $100 while passing through Japan en route to Brazil. With this amount, Alec's father had purchased a pearl necklace meant to comfort his wife who was depressed to be leaving her home in Taiwan.

In letters from Brazil, we were soon asked to pay $600 to a Brazilian realtor for the title to a restaurant and boarding house in Sao Paolo. The realtor had been promised that a son in America would be committed to pay this amount. Alec was enraged by this dictate and refused to meet the gentleman when he arrived at the Chicago airport to collect the money. Hours later we had to face the realtor's anger when he appeared at our apartment door, demanding the promised payment.

His anger abated and he became more reasonable when he realized that we lived in a studio apartment only and had a baby on the way. He saw that living in America did not mean we were rich. Alec did not pay the requested sum, and from then on we had no more direct demands to send money to Brazil—only mail from disappointed parents.

As time passed, I realized that Alec's mind remained burdened with the fate of his parents, especially with their heavy debt that his brother had taken on his shoulders. Yet, I knew Alec had forged his own education and livelihood from his early teens in three different countries, losing much of his health on the way. He now deserved a peaceful family life, also for the sake of his wife and children in the future. Yet every letter from Brazil and Taiwan continued to cause great anxiety for both of us. To lighten the increasing tension between us, Alec asked me, "Let me handle the situation in the Chinese way." What is the Chinese way to avoid conflict? I wondered and only gradually found out: "Never refuse directly, remain positive, but find alternate means to solve the problem."

An additional concern developed during our early weeks of marriage that made that time so stressful. Before our engagement, Alec informed me that he had some form of painful arthritis for which he had received medical attention when he lived in Japan. When I noticed that he took a lot of pain medication, I suggested that he go through an intensive health examination at Mayo Clinic in Rochester, Minnesota. A specialist at Mayo diagnosed his pain as *Ankilosis Spondylitis,* a progressive inflammation of the spine that gradually stiffens and bends downward the posture of the body. Continued pain medication was prescribed, as well as exercises to maintain flexibility. The physician speculated that Alec's deprivation and demanding style of life had called forth a development that was already imprinted in his DNA structure.

In spite of these problems, our life together was happy. We liked to philosophize and enjoyed modest, practical ventures. We spent time with friends and we loved our work and studies. For me, Alec's physical suffering brought a shadow into our lives more immediate than those coming from abroad, shadows that also might reach into the life of our joyfully expected child.

CHAPTER 18

A DELAYED HONEYMOON IN WISCONSIN

Alec had finished his Master's degree and I was in my third month of pregnancy when we visited Annie Voigtritter, Alec's former landlady in Chicago. We were received with open arms, as always. She was homebound in a wheelchair then, but she and Alec shared memories of past trips to Fries Lake, where she still owned a large cottage. Annie's husband, an architect, had built the cottage in the Chinese style. During his visits, Alec's interests had often been divided between fishing, exploring the architecture of the cottage, and relaxing with the family's gentle dog, a large Saint Bernard.

At a quiet point in the conversation, Annie said, "Alec, would you and Ursula want to spend a belated honeymoon at our cottage on Fries Lake during summer break? You know the area and how to run the house. We would be happy to have you look after it." She surprised us both. Sitting next to the Saint Bernard, Alec looked at me with a hopeful smile and, seeing a positive nod, accepted the offer with enthusiasm and gratitude. Annie's daughter, also named Ursula, was a nutritionist for American Airlines and she at once promised some of her special recipes for our kitchen and a weekend visit with the dog, who liked the freedom to run at Fries Lake.

Alec described to me the beauty of the summer home, remembering evenings with glowing logs in the fireplace and stories about the day's fishing. After all those fishing trips with Mr. Hiakawa, here was a chance to stay right next to the lake and give me a much needed rest from teaching.

I looked forward to this escape out of the big city and felt strong and confident during my last weeks at the Latin School, where I enjoyed the questioning learners, the humor of a very companionable faculty, and a supportive headmaster. Now, however, I was mostly concerned about the baby growing in my body. This was my first pregnancy, and age 38 seemed rather late for a birth without problems. My female physician had warned, "Why did you select a natural birth? Just choose sedation and avoid the pain." With this, I remembered my mother's descriptions of her own difficult struggle to bring me into the world; maybe that was why I'd been an only child. In spite of it all, I insisted that I wanted to be awake for the birth experience.

The topic of childbirth was also being discussed in the Latin School teachers' lounge, in response to my concerned questions. Somehow we got all involved in the ever-lasting and hostile discussions between the atheist bachelor mathematics teacher, Charles, and the humorous English teacher, Dick, who would eventually become a priest. On that day, Charles criticized Catholic Church doctrine that confined unbaptized stillborn babies to limbo instead of heaven. Dick quickly replied, "We avoid that situation by having the mother drink holy water for baptism in utero. This will keep access to heaven open."

Charles, knowing that he was the object of a clever joke, left the teacher's room and the laughing faculty, banging the door behind him.

***

Our ten-day vacation at Fries Lake had all the relaxation of a honeymoon but for me it was more of a babymoon as I adjusted to the double role of wife and mother-to-be. I remember my occasional sadness that my parents in Germany would be deprived of watching their grandchild grow. I also wondered what a new member of the family would mean for Alec and I as a couple.

During our stay we enjoyed boating and fishing, especially at sunset and the gentleness of evening time. One evening Alec brought a large carp into the kitchen with the idea to prepare it in a different way to remove the "earthy" taste with vegetables. Again, we were not too pleased with the outcome. "Baby also rejects the taste of carp dinners," I said to him.

Roasting marshmallows in the evening over an outdoor fire was another experience we had not known as foreigners. Ursula Voigtritter provided the recipe and technique, and the Saint Bernard begged eagerly for his portion.

The cottage neighbors had advised that the Basilica of Mary, a national shrine, was a central tourist attraction in Wisconsin. With much expectation, we drove up part of the hill and decided to walk the rest — not a good choice on a hot summer day. But the walk rewarded us with a red-gold setting sun and the light- and shadow-bathed valley. We learned that a

French diary and map had led a French hermit, Subiro, onto this summit, where he had found an altar and a cross. A second hermit took residence there in 1882. His presence attracted Irish and German immigrants who erected a large wooden cross on top of the Hill, reminding all that this was a holy place. With the help of many German settlers, this became "The Shrine of Mary," and was placed into a basilica, under the directive of the Discalced (barefoot) Carmelites of Bavaria, who still today are in charge of the hill. We stopped at the monastery for refreshments and then walked back to the car with satisfaction. What I could not express to Alec was that this highly admired building could not compare with the Cathedral of Cologne, or the Basilica of St. Ursula, or The Apostles Romanesque Church in Cologne, buildings I longingly remembered.

CHAPTER 19

TOWARD A TEACHING CAREER

In winter 1963, Alec and I met with Father Hecht, S.J. in his office. He shook Alec's hand in congratulations and joy, both for our marriage and for Alec's academic achievement of the Master's in Philosophy. Father Hecht took time to chat with us, mentioning colleges currently looking for instructors of philosophy. "These days many priests who have left their professions apply for such positions. You will have some competition," he reminded Alec. "You will be lucky to find preference for a lay professional." He ended the cordial visit with some advice, "From now on, no more money for your parents to Brazil. Your profession and your future family must take priority." This was a comment that I would carry in my heart over the years to come.

Alec's third college interview led us to Viterbo, a small women's college in La Crosse, Wisconsin. The Burlington railroad carried us away from Chicago and held us agape, with almost ecstatic joy, when it snaked along extended stretches of the Mississippi River. Yes, we would love to live in the vicinity of such beauty.

In La Crosse, Pat Sheehan, a representative of the college, met us at the station and showed us around the campus. It was small in comparison to the big city universities, but very neat and inviting. The interview with the college president, Sister Justille, and dean of students, Sister Mynette, went smoothly. Alec left a strong impression of his courageous intercultural experiences as foundations for his philosophical questioning. A week later, he received a job offer for instructor in philosophy, with a salary hardly more than his railroad job had offered. He accepted with the additional assurance that Sister Grace, head of the nursing department, would assist me with birth questions and that the college-related St. Francis Hospital would offer expert obstetric care.

An apartment was secured in the only high-rise in town, just two blocks from the college. We arranged transport from Chicago for our bedding and furniture, but the rest of our possessions — mostly books — were packed into our blue Ford until the car's hind quarters appeared to sag toward the ground.

I resigned from my beloved Latin School and surrendered a grant for a French summer workshop. With a heavy-hearted farewell to our friends in Chicago, we started our new venture. It appeared to us like a magic fairyland experience. We stood in amazement at the Standing Rock Monument on the Wisconsin River. At Lake Geneva, we admired the luxurious accommodations and entertainments for tourists, and we stayed overnight at a modest motel.

While driving further north, I noticed more needle wood and scraggly little bushes that seemed to indicate a colder "Nordic" climate in the Wisconsin Dells region. We stayed there the second night and enjoyed the boat ride through the Dells that refreshed memories of our first, pre-nuptial trip to this beautiful place.

On the last stretch of the trip, our sturdy and reliable car showed signs of weariness and started shaking like a boat on restless water. Right in front of a gas station, a back tire sagged into flatness and almost pulled the book-packed rear to the ground. It was magic, indeed, that we were in front of a repair shop. We did not even have to unload all the books to get the tire inflated. Light-hearted and grateful, we arrived in La Crosse, where the Franciscan sisters invited us to spend the first night at the college since our furniture would not arrive until the following day.

When we moved into the Cass Street Apartments, I was seven months pregnant. The one-bedroom "mansion" on third floor was comfortable, and I was now ready to meet Dr. Amando Alonso at the St. Francis Hospital. He promised he would help me toward a natural childbirth, which had been discouraged in Chicago.

Coming from the restless metropolis, with the city's intense traffic, we approached the more sedate Wisconsin town with much contentment.

CHAPTER 20

FAMILY LIFE IN LA CROSSE

When the first day of classes approached, Alec was worried and nervous. I had suffered the same feelings at the beginning of every school year during my teaching career. Yet, his concerns seemed more justified than mine, when he wondered aloud, "Will I be accepted as the only foreign instructor in this all-white college? Does this community still hold the traditional American view of the 'Chinese *coolie?*' Will students complain about my accent? Will I find the right approach for an all-female audience of both sisters and lay women?"

In Chicago these concerns hardly arose, but La Crosse was a community of fifty thousand citizens, separated by extensive fields and forests, more than one hundred miles from the next urban area. Having spent six years in Chicago, neither Alec nor I had any insight into rural and small-town living. Yet, Alec's vast intercultural insights became a special treasure in La Crosse. He wove them into his lectures, linking abstract philosophical concepts to life here and now, holding students' attention.

Considering the students' rural backgrounds, there was little foundation they brought to the subject of philosophy. Courses in theology and philosophy were required in Catholic colleges, and students were sometimes resentful of having to take these "extras," especially those women preparing for careers in nursing.

Once Alec had paved his way into the college community, curiosity and questioning also arose about me, his German wife, soon to produce a racially mixed baby. Curiosity about our marriage was lively among the neighbors, since the town had no other biracial couples. From the questions asked, we understood very quickly whether our union was accepted or deemed a faux pas.

Curiosity about the arrival of a biracial child really exploded at the birth of our son, Marcel, on Halloween, 1963. Most of the teaching Sisters of the college came to the hospital and visited the new baby, along with a great number of Alec's students. Little Marcel was on exhibit close to the large nursery window, showing off his full shock of black hair and, occasionally, his big brown eyes. In my hospital room, visitors talked away some of my much needed rest, and Marcel was too small to appreciate the attention paid him by the public. Did he appreciate his mother's twelve hours of labor that brought him to daylight? My efforts had been so painful that, in the end, Dr. Armando cancelled my attempt at natural birth and administered sedatives. Yet, I experienced, in consciousness, that there was no greater joy than holding a small newborn baby in motherly embrace. Discomfort and pain were soon forgotten over the miracle of a new life.

My hospital roommate—a white woman who gave birth to a little girl—kept close watch of the attention given to me and my baby. Hers was also a biracial baby—from her union with a Winnebago Indian from the Wisconsin Dells—but there were no parents, siblings, or friends to congratulate her. So intent was she on the events going on around my bed, that later she remembered names and parts of conversations among my many visitors. I was sad that I could only extend friendly words to her, but hardly share the same care and attention I had received.

After three days in the hospital, baby Marcel and I were discharged. It was no easy task to quiet a distressed baby in the apartment, especially when the neighbors expressed anger by knocking on the ceiling. I had insufficient milk so the pediatrician suggested bottle feeding and soon we entered a peaceful, enjoyable relationship. I had much to learn, and limited help, although the rocking chair Alec bought gave both Marcel and me hours of intimacy.

After two weeks Rev. Father Joseph Blank, S.J., who had blessed our wedding, called from St. Louis. He had promised to baptize Marcel, and said it was now urgent due to his declining health. We selected Thanksgiving as the day for baptism and met Uncle Joseph, supported by a Jesuit brother, at the train station. Monsignor Kundinger, at the cathedral, kindly hosted the visitors overnight. To our regret, Richard Dolezal, the godfather, was unable to attend the baptism, and Jim Larson, Alec's colleague, generously offered to substitute. When Marcel received the waters of baptism and his name, Marcel Heinrich (his middle name that of my father), he was dressed in a baptismal garment made by the Sisters and he tolerated the holy water on his head without protest. We were a family.

Alec was so proud of his baby boy, and I thought I had accomplished the best event of my life.

It was not so with my hospital roommate. Weeks later she appeared at our apartment, asking to see my baby. What a difference between Marcel, sleeping in contentment, and her straggly, poorly nourished daughter. She asked me for baby food, which I gave her knowing I could purchase more the next day. Weeks later she came again asking for money to pay her rent, which I did not give her having already stowed some clothing, diapers, and food in her basket. Several weeks later, she returned with her husband who wanted to know how he could get a job at Viterbo College like my husband. I became anxious when they stayed for hours, disregarding my suggestion to leave after a meal. "I like it here," her husband said, "where can I get an apartment like this?" When Alec returned home and announced that we had an appointment at the college, they understood that it was time to leave.

Several months later, she returned and said she had been in the hospital after her husband had beaten her. This time, I needed to find more help and called Monsignor Kundinger at the Catholic Social Services, where the couple and their needs were already known. They asked me to send her to their office. From there, she and her baby would be sent back to the reservation where more aid could be given. I often wondered what life was like for her and her baby in the following years. From Viterbo nurses, I learned of a second baby and more beatings, but there was no further contact with our family.

When I held my baby close I frequently thought, *Marcel, do you know how lucky you are to be born to us rather than to the parents of the baby who shared our hospital room?*

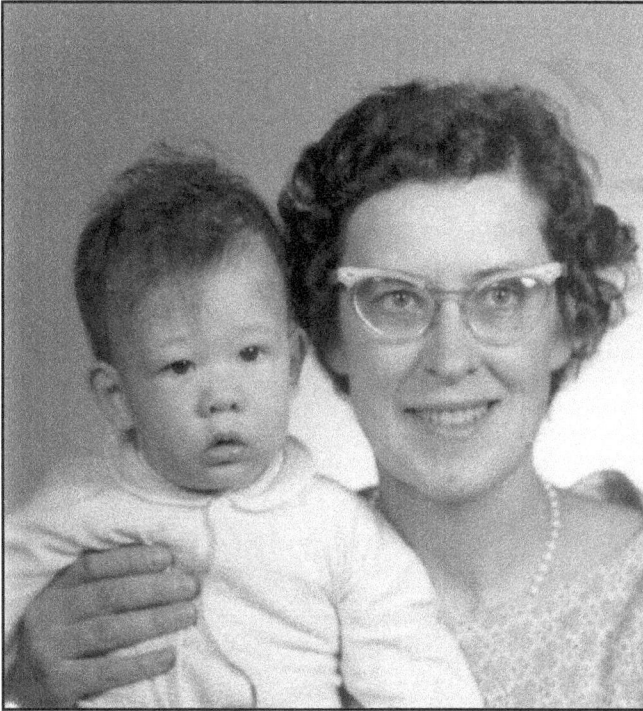

Baby Marcel and Ursula, 1963.

CHAPTER 21

THE GIFT OF CHILDREN

When the Sisters at the college learned that we were trying
to find an apartment on the ground level, the Viterbo college
administration offered Siena Hall. A small, former student residence, Siena Hall was now closed due to a planned expansion
of the college. The offer of this space appeared to be a good
choice for us, even though the building was far below the German standards of "Wohnkultur" (cultured living).

On the exterior, neglected dark green clapboard was offset
with equally rundown white window frames. Inside, the two-
story home featured spacious rooms with old-fashioned wall-
paper and plain, creaky wooden floors with steep stairs leading
to the second floor. There was no fashionable wooden elegance
that I had dreamed of long ago, but it had room to breathe, to
play, and to let our Pekinese dog, Cho-Cho, run around. Luck-
ily, Marcel was not at the climbing stage yet. We appreciated
the slanting porch with its easy access to the big lawn, sandbox, and cherry tree. All of this was "child heaven" and more
open to visitors than apartment living.

In our new home, Alec loved to place Marcel on a lap pillow
and play melodies on his mund harmonica (mouth organ) that
reminded him of Hong Kong. Later, he would lie on the floor

and move the red truck, the first toy he had given to his first son, who was now the pride of his life. Gradually, this toy was followed by a circus wagon with animals in cages, then a large box with wooden blocks and Playschool toys. I was impressed and delighted to see Alec's practical skills in baby care— including dirty diapers—and later on with creative play skills.

Two years later when Monica was ready to join the family, her petite body came via a fast birth. Dr. Armando made sure that I could watch her natural birth, which I did with great joy. Alec missed it, since he could not be reached while teaching, but soon accepted "his girl" with equal joy. My friend and fellow teacher Ellie Lambrakis arrived from Chicago for the baptism. I was so thankful and proud to have this learned and loving woman as Monica's godmother. I had been equally pleased when Dick Dolezal had agreed to be Marcel's godfather two years earlier. He was another outstanding teacher with a searching mind as a teacher of literature and a searcher for spiritual values.

In July, two months after Monica's birth, we returned to Fries Lake where we had honeymooned. In her pink and white lace-decorated basket, Monica was hardly aware of the changed environment while Marcel enjoyed the garden and lake water that apartment life had long denied him. For Alec, fishing was a great release during those tense years as a beginning teacher, and from the strain of "being different" within an overwhelmingly German-Norwegian community.

When Alec joined the college as a lay instructor of philosophy, the departments of chemistry, history, and art were also occupied by lay instructors; he was the fourth. Alec discovered that he had different students from those he had studied with in Chicago. At that time, all of the college students were lay women, with a sprinkling of Sisters who completed their degrees after years of teaching. Philosophical questioning was far from the experience of many students coming from rural areas, and so was the use of philosophical terminology. The highly motivated students appreciated his classes, even if they seemed to not relate directly to their professional goals. Because philosophy was a required subject, however, some less-motivated students complained, "We do not understand the instructor's accent. He is too foreign. What is philosophy good for, anyway?" They masked their reluctance to study in depth with these excuses.

Alec worked many hours into the night developing new, sometimes entertaining, approaches to his subject to make philosophy more accessible. His position within the campus community was greatly strengthened when the college developed a presentation on Eastern cultures in which Alec and the students from Japan and China were invited to share their cultural knowledge and rituals. The workshop was a great success.

For Alec and me, it brought the valuable and delightful friendship of five students from Japan and China, and also moved our whole family closer into the academic community of Viterbo College. The foreign students were delighted when they could drop-in on our family life just across the street from their lecture halls. With us they could speak their own languages, find cultural understanding, and get help with their English papers. They loved to play with the children, and I learned many useful recipes from them.

When Michael was born, two years after Monica, he weighed almost ten pounds. This time Dr. Alonzo had encouraged Alec to be by my side during the birth. Our student friends visited almost daily, especially Yuki Shibuta from Japan. They kept our older children busy, rocked and strolled with the baby, and lent a hand in the household wherever needed.

Life in Siena Hall was a happy time for us, even when Marcel tumbled down the steep back stairs, Monica painted her bedroom wall with dirt, and the John Birch Society neighbors called the police to our house. The neighbors accused our children of dishonoring the flag — the little paper American flags that they had planted on crumbling forts in their sandbox. The policeman just smiled and advised us to keep the flags out of the neighbor's view. ChoCho, the dog, must have thought revenge was in order for he crawled under the neighbor's fence and dug out some of the Birchers' flowers. Since there were other dogs in the neighborhood, he could not easily be accused.

In spite of the additional complaints, the whole family was sad when we had to return ChoCho to the animal shelter for his refusal to learn obedience and cleanliness etiquette, especially in housetraining.

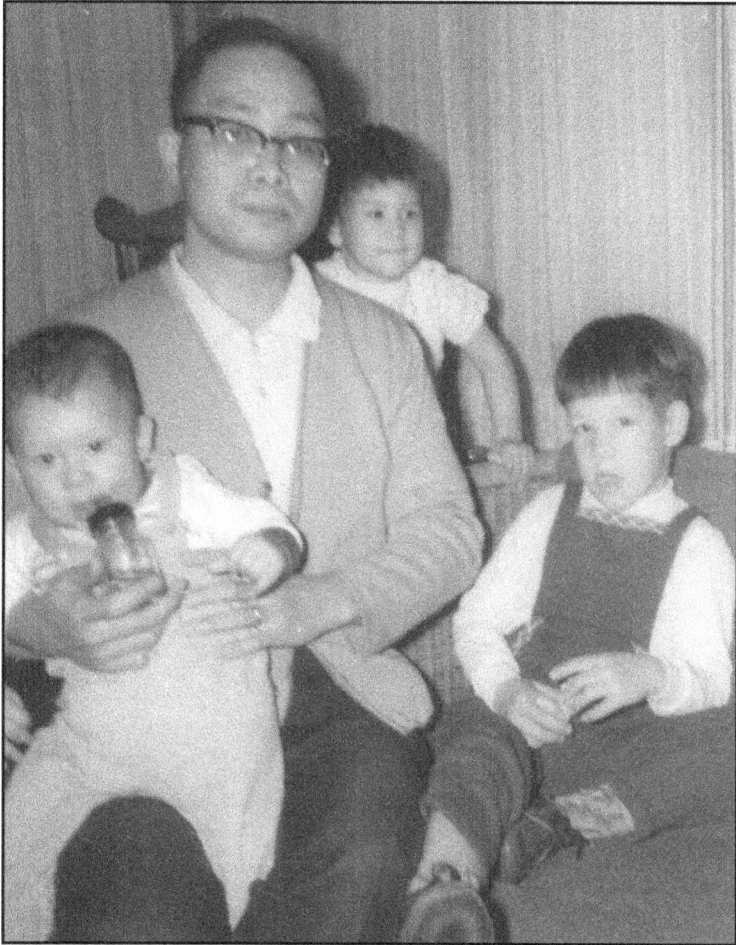

Baby Michael, Monica, and Marcel with their father, 1967.

CHAPTER 22

NEW HOMES OF OUR OWN

The decision to search for a house of our own was hastened by college building plans for a large fine arts center. The whole block of buildings was to be razed, so we bade farewell to Siena Hall, home of much joy and peace.

With Alec's good sense of organization, business, and decisiveness, we soon found a home near the University of La Crosse. The building had housed a family with six children and certainly was big enough for us. Located on a grassy slope, it looked majestic with its white plaster walls and brown window frames, all in a Dutch colonial style. From the small backyard, the university buildings were visible and less than a block away.

From the entrance, the spacious home interior offered immediate access to the living room, which could be closed by a glass sliding door or extended by use of an indoor porch with many windows. A smaller room, off the living room, was Alec's immediate choice for an office. On the left of the hallway, the dining room abutted a small kitchen, alas, a bit too narrow for two cooks. The green speckled carpeting on the first floor made this area warm and comfortable, while the second floor had polished wooden floorboards and rugs. A wood-crafted staircase, wide enough to accommodate three kids in a row, led to three bedrooms expansive enough to provide sleep and play areas for the children, and private sleeping quarters for Alec and me. The large unfinished basement housed a laundry room and furnace, leaving enough space for kids' tricycle rides around the utility boxes.

The home was just right for our family plans: Marcel could walk to the university's Lab School Kindergarten. With my part-time teaching position at the university, I could walk with him to school. Alec, who had decided to finish his doctorate in Madison, came home on weekends only. For little Michael, and to help with household duties, we hired Betty, who had raised her own four children and done housekeeping work at Viterbo. She also owned a car, necessary to transport Monica to the Montessori school. At this point in my life, I still had not earned my driver's license because I had not felt the need for it.

We were soon at home in this warm and comfortable house. Marcel brought home his artwork from Mrs. Peterson's class. His "Rickety-Rackety Rooster" drawing is still a priceless decoration on my living room wall. The pet hamsters we kept in the basement were short-lived after one of them killed her babies.

A little boy named Pete, from the busy family next door, took a liking to our family and the pets. He would ring the front door bell at eight in the morning, or even earlier. We had to tell him that he was no longer allowed to come up the four steps to the front door until he was invited. "Not to the front door," he said, "but by law I can stand on the sidewalk."

Mrs. Schubert, the wealthy retired lady from the kitty-corner mansion, liked to invite us for tea because she thought the children were "so cute." She was not the only one expressing these thoughts. Often a stranger would stop us with a variety of curious comments and questions: "What darling kids! Such cute eyes! Where do they come from? Are they from here? Are you their grandmother? They look so different — from another country? Are they adopted?" I never explained my children's origin, and instead gave non-committal responses or walked away wordless and mad about these strangers' insensitive questions. I was bothered by public curiosity, but also proud of my own delightful, vibrant children who reveled in people's attention.

I finished teaching by three o'clock, and Betty would have the kids ready for the afternoon adventure. We settled Mike in his stroller with Marcel and Monica "helping" or holding on to both handles. Myrick Park was our favorite destination, with the children hoping for another ride on the merry-go-round boats or an ice cream cone from the concession stand. We fed our dry bread to each child's favorite animal: Marcel hand-fed the deer; Monica threw pieces to the monkeys in response to their inviting gestures; Michael dropped his pieces into the duck pond, then hid behind my back when the flock paddled to the shore with a greedy Canada Goose in the lead.

We celebrated the weekends, when Alec came home. There was a special meal for him, cookies baked with the kids' eager hands, children's block architecture on display in the play room, and school work. Betty deserved a special compliment for having the house in good order and the kids clean, safe, and well-fed. As for the adults, we stuck to our own cooking over Betty's "mish-mash" productions, to quote the children.

On some of these weekends, Alec returned to catching bluegills, and occasionally small salmon and whitefish, until Marcel, at age seven, made a catch that became the family trophy and was never outdone by his dad, who celebrated the master-catch with his son.

On a trip to visit my parents in Germany, I was able to take Monica along and found her to be a compliant, entertaining co-traveler. "I'm not afraid," she whispered to me on the plane, and clung with white knuckles to her protective objects. Naturally, her grandparents and all of our relatives were delighted with her quick spirit and cute appearance. She took great interest in her grandfather's goldsmith studio filled with polishing machines, old jewelry, and tools. She learned about different fruit trees in Grandpa's mini orchard and dug out carrots with her grandmother. On Sunday, we planned to take a walk — my parents had a stroller that we had used on a previous visit when Marcel was only eight months old — but when the time came to leave Monica became a screaming bundle huddled in the hallway crying, "Not that stroller, I want my home one." Finally, she agreed to push the foreign stroller until, exhausted, she agreed to climb inside and be pushed.

***

We spent three happy years in that first house, always expecting that it would be bought by the university as we had been informed at the time of purchase. When plans were finalized, the university offered a substantial amount of money for us to put toward a new house. This time, we searched for a home in the suburbs with plenty of lawn space in a neighborhood with many children and a good school nearby.

Our new home was a modern split-level house with four bedrooms, a basement that could be finished, and a spacious backyard with four large spruce trees, a birch, and a sprawling crabapple tree. Some flower beds were planted with perennials, which reminded me of my mother's garden. Near the garage grew another spruce that—along with the two maples in front of the building—provided comfort in both summer and winter. A small park across the street would be changed into a skating pond in winter. State Road School, La Crosse's newest, was a ten-minute walk along Pammel Creek. Now we had it all: a modern home, front and back yards, a park, friendly neighbors and their children.

***

"You need to learn the secrets of driving," Alec said one day, after we had settled in to our new house. "You will want to be flexible and able to follow your own interests when the children and I are at school." Alec remained always concerned that I have my own space and interests beyond the care of the family and household. This was an unusual trait, as a traditional Chinese husband would expect his wife to be selflessly devoted to the family's needs only. Alec had observed many different styles of family living that had altered and deepened his view of married relationship to more generous alternatives beyond the traditional Confucian type.

I followed Alec's suggestion that I learn to drive and have enjoyed driving ever since he surprised me with a used blue Chevy after I had obtained my driver's license. Years later, he bought a brand-new red Toyota Corolla for my birthday.

We found compatible community on Twenty-Ninth Street, where Alec's permanent anxiety of not being accepted was quickly dispersed. We experienced an early welcome when two neighboring weekend fishermen invited Alec to accompany them to their choice fishing grounds.

Mr. Morgan and his family, across the street, was always ready to go fishing, or to give advice and help with house-related problems. Monica soon gathered Mary, Karen, Shelley, and the Knudsen girls as same-age friends, who were also willing to include four-year-old Mike in their group. Marcel found himself invited to play board games in the Kuhls' garage, with *Risk* — the struggle for world domination — as their favorite game. Brian McNurlen contributed to the fun with shows for the neighborhood children in his family's backyard tent. Dr. Murphy's family, with eleven children, three houses down from ours, was always active with various sports in the park across from our house. Eventually, when Mike joined the neighborhood crowd going to State Road School, he found a good friend and fellow-biker in Paul Gustafson.

Summer neighborhood gatherings in the park meant "food fest and fun," where we cautiously tried Mr. Miller's turtle stew. It was a delicacy, but we could not dismiss from our minds the memory of a big turtle we had carried off the road in Goose Island to save it from the traffic even though it had peed on my dress.

The house on Twenty-Ninth Street, La Crosse, Wisconsin.

Friends in La Crosse.

Alec and Ursula with their children and Ursula's mother, Mrs. Elisabeth Blank.

CHAPTER 23

ATTEMPTS AT CAMPING

When my father died in Germany in 1973, I wanted to be present at his funeral. My mother needed support, and I wanted to show my deep gratitude and to honor him one last time. My father never had a son to call his own, so I was sure he would appreciate the presence of a male grandchild at his last rites. Mike was four years old at the time, and the only one who had not yet met my parents. I knew he would be thrilled to travel by plane to Cologne and see the grandparents and the cathedral I had talked about so often. Mike snatched his latest take-apart toy car and was ready on the spot upon hearing our plans of flying to Germany.

It was the beginning of summer vacation so Alec would stay behind and take care of Marcel, age ten, and Monica, eight, both of whom had become quite independent by this time. Alec immediately had a vision of how to spend the time in our absence. After we left, he explored the Army Surplus store for a spacious, solid, five-person tent. He had the guidance of his friend Joe Motivans, who was an experienced camper with his five children.

Since Alec enjoyed fishing, he chose a spot on the Lake Superior coast as his goal, nearly three hundred miles to the north. Fishing gear, clothes, and swimming outfits were packed quickly and stored in the back of the Volkswagen station wagon. With great enthusiasm, Marcel and Monica added toys and books and let the neighborhood know about the details of packing. None of our good neighborhood friends thought of letting the immigrant family know that the climate and environment hundreds of miles to the north would be different and rougher.

The kids' enthusiasm lasted through the long drive, especially since Alec had the talent and creative energy to bring up new and entertaining ideas along the way. Among them were stops by brooks or other bodies of water where the kids were encouraged to look for worms. On this task they cooperated with reluctant enthusiasm because they knew that worms led to fish and to Dad's Chinese fish-ball soups, which were not their favorites. But Alec encouraged them by saying, "Lake Superior fish might be tastier than those in the Mississippi River." Marcel chimed in with his research that in some places in Lake Superior fish could be seen as deep as one hundred feet down. Monica—with her interest in beautiful, artistic things— had learned that the sandstone bluffs contained many agates, semi-precious stones that she might use in her crafts. The kids had also discovered that Lake Superior was the world's largest and cleanest freshwater lake. The fact that ninety percent of its shoreline was uninhabited they could hardly imagine.

After a stop-over in Minneapolis, they turned north toward Bayfield, where they learned that Indian tribes had originally named the great lake, Gitchee Gumee. "Does that mean they make gum there?" they asked their dad with anticipation.

Disregarding the commercial camping grounds along the shore, Alec stopped at an isolated rocky coast and chose this spot for the tent. They set it up together, then the children ran to the water where they found rotting tree branches turned white from changing temperatures. At closer inspection, they discovered that the branches were covered with thousands of red and black ladybugs. "Could Dad use those for fishing?" they wondered. They ran back to inform their dad, and also to get warmer clothing to protect them against the evening wind. Alec did not think fish had ever tasted hard-winged bugs since those did not live in lake water. As to warmer clothes, there were none; La Crosse had been sunny and quite hot. He gave the kids his jacket. Even at night in the tent the cool temperatures robbed them of relaxing sleep as Alec had forgotten to pack sleeping bags! The kids slept in the tent; Alec spent the night in the Volkswagen.

A morning fire, using wood pieces and the frying pan from home for making eggs, was exciting. The children explored along the coast while Alec tried his fishing line with the surviving worms. Climbing and investigating along the coast entertained the children until it started raining. What to do now? They sat and read in the tent for a while, followed by a quick trip to the neighboring town, after which a drive along the lake brought them into a larger town that featured a movie theater.

The movie *Jaws* had just come out that summer. Though unknown to Alec at the time, the film told "the story of a man-eating white shark who terrorizes a beach community." The children, with enthusiasm, begged to see the film they had heard so much about. Alec, rather uneasy, but having no alternative for entertainment in the rain, agreed to attend the show. That night in the tent led to a retreat back into the Volkswagen because frightening pictures of sharks with wide-open toothy jaws were alive in the children's dreams, and would be many times in the future.

The third night was spent at a commercial campground that offered more amenities, and opportunities to play with other children, but no nearby fishing spot to satisfy Alec's original vision. After a three-day trip, they returned to La Crosse, eager to share their camping adventures.

When Michael and I returned from Germany, the kids' report about their camping trip on Lake Superior sounded so exciting and worthwhile that we were made to feel outdone.

One of Alec's master catches.

CHAPTER 24

THE STREET COMMUNITY

Alec spent many hours on home improvements after his friends and neighbors had encouraged him to translate his ideas into tangible achievements. "We need more room to accommodate kids on rainy days," Alec decided one day, and went to task wood-paneling the basement to create a play-room. Some of the neighbors said, "We'll be there to advise you. We did our own long ago." I admired Alec for investing himself in physical labor, so opposite the image of a bookish scholar.

With surprise and pride Alec discovered that he had an effi-cient and reliable helper in little Michael who, at ten years old, assisted him with the paneling. He would marvel, "Mike is able to help nail in wood panels, plan window frames, and he can stick to the job for hours." A shared pizza was often the reward. Michael's bottomless stomach and unusual growth-spurt caused him to be pizza-hungry at any time. Marcel, mean-while, preferred to play sports outside and war-games with the two boys next door though he would later turn toward books and science.

Alec put eager effort into his constructions. He was demanding and precise, and happy when the boys would help him. They also dared to nail shingles, under their dad's guidance, when a new roof was needed. The removal of two large, messy plum trees from the front lawn pulled family members, neighbors, advice-givers, and on-lookers together and offered much excitement for the children, who gathered small branches for a toy cabin. Alec also built a larger back porch with a stairway into the back yard, all with Joe Motivan's help.

Our two elderly yet active neighbors sold their home to a family from India: Mr. Kulas Sarker, his wife Manju, and son Tuplu. The new family was surprised that a professor like Alec would do "menial work" in his home. Kulas, an engineer, watched Alec's projects and attempted his own backyard improvement. A heap of bricks was deposited on his driveway, and — under his supervision — his wife carried the bricks in place and laid out flower beds. Mr. Kulas' male dignity did not allow him to help his wife with this "low-class job." Occasionally, neighbors made gentle comments that failed to activate the husband to help. Neighborhood women advised Manju to leave the heavy labor to her husband, and we made sure she understood how to go about it. Manju, a well-educated accountant, did not succeed in changing her husband, but she enjoyed our female support. Many years later, after their family moved to Chicago, we learned that Manju had become the sole bread-winner when her husband fell ill and was no longer able to work.

Alec's basement project had been so successful that he next tried his hand at a playhouse for the children. On a large wooden platform behind the garage, the playhouse—big enough to hold ten kids—had two windows and split upper/lower doors. With much excitement, the kids of the neighborhood took possession of the building. Now, the Chius were fully anchored in the neighborhood.

With the new playhouse, five neighborhood girls decided to open their own "school" for younger kids on the street. They kept busy designing textbooks and lesson plans for reading, writing, math, gym, and art. Parents were informed of the plan for "Sunshine School" and were quite happy to know their little ones were busy and safe. The project ran with great enthusiasm on the part of "teachers" and tutees, who were developing pre-school to first grade skills for three hours every day. "Regular attendance is highly recommended," the teachers reminded the parents. Tuition was five cents per child, and lunch consisted of dry cereal, no milk.

The Sunshine School was so popular that a journalist from the local newspaper took pictures and interviewed the kids. The article in the *La Crosse Tribune* expressed admiration and praise for work done by the originators of the Sunshine School. It also challenged other neighborhoods to copy the experiment.

A group of children several blocks away opened their own "school" too, but charged a dollar per kid. They copied the idea and also earned money for something that was a joy in itself, which provoked white-hot wrath in the original organizers. They came close to writing a complaint in the newspaper, but soon their own new ideas made them forget the copy-cat program.

Other creative endeavors included a dance-and-song pro-duction on the playhouse deck for the neighbors and an "Art

Show on the Green," displaying drawings hung on a rope between two trees in front of our house. Parents received invitations to vote for the best piece of art on display. When Karen Kuhl won "Best of Show" with her "Disney Snoopy Dog," Monica was deeply disappointed that her original drawings, illustrating a collection of her own short stories, did not garner any awards.

I had been teaching part-time at the university's German Department since 1969, but in 1972 the department experienced a decline of students and my support was no longer needed. I was concerned about my ability to add to the family income and the financial pressure from Alec's family reminded me that I wanted to maintain some financial independence. An offer to teach French and German at the local high school did not materialize, since the district could not afford the salary they would have to pay. A counselor in the Education Department suggested I focus on Special Education, which was in high demand at that time. With much support from Alec and the kids, I graduated with an MA in Special Education in 1975 and found a teaching position immediately. I chose to work part-time in an elementary school although I had no experience teaching children of this age. I loved teaching — working with children and youths of any level — but working with the younger ages and with problem learners was a great challenge for me. My first love remained the teaching of foreign languages, which I continued with some gifted students in my spare time.

At the same time, Alec had completed his requirements for the Ph.D. in Philosophy and needed to focus on his dissertation. "I do not know if my health can stand any further stress," he often worried. Pain from the spinal inflammation was merciless and needed to be controlled daily by Indocine. This powerful medication caused bleeding stomach ulcers that required extra medical attention. Alec tried to steel his body with regular, punishing exercises on the treadmill. In his office he kept strict study hours, listening to classical music and drinking only glasses of water for relief. Among his colleagues, hardly anyone realized his daily bouts with pain.

Our finished basement and the playhouse satisfied the Chiu children's needs, but after those projects Alec began taking cabinet-making classes at the Technical Institute. Joe Motivans had already contributed much to Alec's wood-crafting enthusiasm and skill development. Along with several university professors, they met at the Institute's workshop each Monday, learning from each other and from experienced wood-working teachers in an atmosphere of jovial exchange, pleasantry, and utmost caution.

I still have a wooden cat on the kitchen wall supporting a china bird. Chinese ideograms of "peace" and "married happiness" set into multi-tinted wood structures soon decorated dining room walls. Mirrors in oak, maple, and walnut frames were welcome in everybody's bedroom. One Christmas, I received a jewelry box, featuring a drawer and compartments laid out with velvet to store precious pieces of jewelry. I'll forever remember Alec's radiant expression when he could surprise me with a new piece he had designed and made at school.

After months and years of learning, the creations became bigger and more intricate; he brought home coffee tables, an oak hope-chest, a china cabinet with glass doors, a chess table with inlaid squares, and cutting boards with elegant designs, too artistic to be used for greasy kitchen tasks.

When the kids were in high school, Alec purchased two, two-story houses that he turned into apartments, using the rental income to add to our family finances. Later, two additional houses were acquired to produce income for Raymond's family in Taiwan. For Alec, repairs in the apartments were demanding, especially since he did most of it himself with some help from the boys.

Eventually, he installed a lathe and a table-saw for woodworking in his garage. On the lathe he turned floor lamps, one for every child, and candle holders that still decorate the altar at Newman Center, the Catholic student center on the campus of the University of Wisconsin, La Crosse. The table-saw came in handy, but was very dangerous. While fixing a window frame in his poorly lit garage, he cut off the upper phalanges of two fingers. As nobody was home at the time, he gathered the stumps and drove himself to Lutheran Hospital. For the rest of his life he thanked Dr. Fink for the expert reconstruction of the severed fingers. Several smaller accidents that followed still did not prevent him from working hastily, and with limited caution.

With his damaged hand, he missed the racquetball games that he regularly played with neighbors Jim Murphy and Ed Morgan, and regretted that he had delayed their weekly enjoyment.

Alec's healing fingers were now also a daily addition to his back pain. Twice he was careless with pain medication. I once found him unconscious in his bed from over-medication and had to call an ambulance. After a night in the hospital, he was well again but angry that I had not just "disregarded the little incident and let him sleep it off."

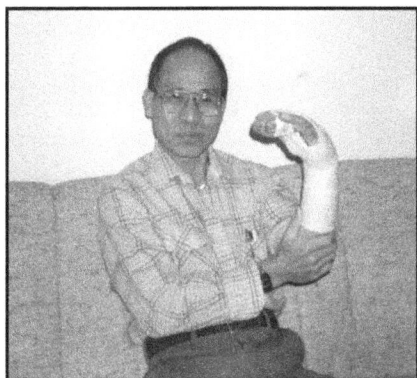

Alec recovering from hand surgery.

CHAPTER 25

BALANCING EASTERN AND WESTERN MOTHERS

Alec's egg rolls and Chinese barbequed chicken became favored dishes among our neighbors and family friends. At home he often prepared fish dinners, using the fish he caught in the river. The kids ate that, but groaned when Chinese fish-ball soup was on the menu. Only reluctantly did they learn to eat it. Their dad was not willing to forgo the delicacies he pulled out of the water. Our family dinners did not always include Chinese dishes; Alec enjoyed any meal except those with lots of potatoes, which reminded him of war-time in China.

His mother had been a good cook, and in peace-time had prepared standard dishes of beef, chicken, pork, or fish, mixed with vegetables, for daily meals. At our home we ate such dishes only at holidays or other special occasions. Alec always helped with these complicated meals, remembering his mother's cooking or improving upon cookbook recipes.

While Alec's eating habits now included American and European dishes, his mother had carried her Chinese cooking techniques to Brazil where she and her husband had established a restaurant. She also gave cooking lessons while his father ran a gift shop next door with items that Raymond sent from Taiwan.

In 1978 Alec's father died suddenly after suffering a stroke. This left Alec's mother to run the business on her own, and she was hampered by her lack of fluency in Portuguese. While suffering with spinal inflammation, Alec flew to Sao Paolo to help his mother with the sale of the properties. She would return to Taiwan, where Raymond would be responsible for her welfare.

Alec knew that I feared nothing as much as a Chinese mother-in-law in our home. The threat of financial requests and interference in our family life remained alive in the back of my mind. Before leaving for Brazil, Alec assured me that he would arrange his mother's flight direct to Taipei.

The Chinese community in Brazil helped out, especially when Alec's health deteriorated due to stress. The sale of the business and official permission for his mother's emigration were delayed beyond Alec's stay in the country. Family friends promised to get his mother ready for departure.

Back in La Crosse, Alec recovered slowly. Raymond kindly repaid the funds for their mother's flight, but informed him that their mother had changed her travel route. "Mother will fly via Chicago," Raymond wrote; "she wants to meet you and the family on the thru-passage to Taipei." At this announcement, my worry increased to almost panic. I feared further complications with Alec's health and the general peaceful living of our family. At this time, Marcel was 15 years old, Monica, 13, and Michael, 11. Alec was still trying to finish his PhD.

How could I reduce his stress over all of these obligations? How could I balance our Western lifestyle against Eastern expectations? I tried to explain to Raymond that Alec's health could not stand much extra worry and pressure. Raymond sent expensive Chinese medicines, such as Tiger Balm, and offered to send him to a spa in Taiwan for relief. Those gestures were kind, but Alec's family never understood the depth of his physical pain and suffering nor his guilt about his inability to support them.

When his mother arrived in Chicago we met her in the airport. There she was, a lonely, but very determined lady. She pressed a fistful of jewelry into my hands, and greeted us all in broken English. Over tea and our initial sharing of news, Alec asked to see her ticket for connecting flights to Taiwan. "I have no ticket. I'll stay here with you," she responded. Alec reminded her of their arrangement in Brazil, of Raymond's preparations for her arrival, and Confucian obligations for widows, but these did not change her mind. Since we were reluctant to draw the children into a rather tense discussion, we called the Baums and asked whether we could meet at their home to discuss the problem while their children and ours played together.

Alec felt even more turmoil than I. He was angry at his mother's disregard of the agreement they had made in Brazil and of his efforts to help her. Although he honored his mother, and felt sorry for her circumstances, he refused to be manipulated into taking on his brother's responsibilities. Raymond had already made living arrangements for their mother in his own home. Alec explained that our family was directed by the two of us and would not be dictated by other family members. When Alec did not invite her to stay with us in La Crosse, his mother called a Chinese family in Chicago who—due to etiquette and a former relationship—offered her a place to stay temporarily. This act was intended to shame Alec and damage his reputation.

In the following weeks and months, the question of what to do about his mother lay heavy on our minds. After many weeks in Chicago, another family from her circle of acquaintances took her in and she moved to Madison. Etiquette obliged them to this kindness, but frequent telephone calls indicated that they expected Alec to be responsible for her. He drove to Madison and explained the problem. We agreed to their suggestion that it would be humiliating for his mother to return to Taiwan without having visited her son in America, so she came to La Crosse to visit for a week. In La Crosse, she revealed her intent to open a restaurant in town for which she had already selected an abandoned McDonald's building and had enlisted a female Chinese cook as a helper. In no uncertain terms, she said, "The children will help with the serving." Alec—very angry at this point—snapped, "In the U.S., children go to school and not to work in restaurants! This family will not support the idea of owning a restaurant." Afterward, Alec purchased plane tickets to Taiwan and arranged for his mother's transportation to the airport. She left without saying a word of farewell.

During his summer vacation, Alec flew to Taipei to consult with his brother about the best arrangement for their disappointed mother. At his arrival, she was not in Raymond's home and nobody knew where she had gone. Weeks later, she wrote to Alec that she had accepted a position as cook and babysitter in the home of a wealthy Chinese family in Los Angeles. Nobody in Raymond's family knew how she had managed this.

The trip to Taipei gave Alec more insight into his brother's life and the family whose welfare had worried him so much over the years. Raymond had paid all of their father's debts and had developed an export business for all kinds of leather gloves that were produced in his own factory. He was quite successful. Looking into the future, however, Alec warned him, "Watch out for competitive Japanese production of the same items. It will, in time, overpower your export markets in Taiwan." His prediction proved correct several years later. Alec always had a good business insight due to his undergraduate specialization in macro- and micro-economics, but he disliked business as a profession because "you cannot be successful without always looking for your own advantage above all, or be successful without cheating," he would explain. For Alec, a teaching career had been the best choice. He loved studying philosophy, his daily class preparations, discussions with colleagues and students, and the extended quiet time in his office.

Much later, we learned a very sad story. After Alec's mother returned to Taipei, she contacted members of her husband's family. During his bankruptcy, her husband had asked his family members to keep a collection of gold bars in hiding. They had agreed that this fund would be for his wife or for building a new business. It seems she had no documents or written agreements of this transaction. When his family denied possession of these valuables, she knew that she had lost face as well as her reputation as a well-to-do woman. Her ability to live independently vanished and she would have to earn her own livelihood.

When we visited her in Los Angeles, she was caring for a seven-year-old boy. We noticed that she only approached the child with orders and blame. The boy followed Alec around instead, with need for affection and encouragement. Alec was unable to make his mother see that—beyond protection and satisfaction of bodily needs—a child longs for acceptance and affection. After termination of this job, his mother briefly returned to Taipei where Raymond and Masako accepted her kindly.

Months later, Alec received a call, "Come and pick me up from Oregon." She had been working for a Chinese dentist there. After a legal struggle over some payments, she found a new position with the family of an American lawyer in Washington D.C. The family employed her as a babysitter and cook, and was highly pleased with her work. Very generous and caring, her new family helped her retrieve the Social Security payments that the Chinese dentist had withheld from her paychecks. They encouraged her to take English language lessons and driver's education, which she did. Alec and the children visited her in Washington, and again several months later in New Jersey where she spent time with relatives. From there, she asked to come home with us to La Crosse because she had been hired as a cook in a Chinese restaurant in Minneapolis. She enjoyed her work and we visited back and forth several times.

Visits with Alec's mother.

When the restaurant moved, she stayed with us in La Crosse. In the evenings, Alec would sit and read his newspaper while his mother expounded upon all kinds of new business ideas in Chinese. Alec couldn't handle it. He was overwhelmed with his teaching and the apartment rentals as it was, and he couldn't make his mother understand that he was not going to support the idea of any type of family business. Worry about her plans and ideas, and hiding these tensions from the kids, created a lot of stress in the household. Over time, I came to appreciate his mother's skillful cooking, her well-regulated days—which included journaling and tai-chi exercises—and her constant concern for relatives. We admired her very inventive planning, though some of her ideas created much turmoil in the family.

Alec suspected that the main reason his mother insisted on living in America was the absence of Chinese social expectations. The refusal of her husband's family to provide the owed funds had depressed her and limited her social and financial prestige in Taiwan. In our discussions about family responsibility, Alec frequently remembered the advice of Father Hecht at Loyola, "Your primary responsibility belongs to your own family," he had said, "and to the maintenance of your health."

Yet his deeper consciousness had not yet fully released his early Confucian understanding of human relationships. He often referred to it in his daily life and in his teaching. The Confucian tradition considers the Chinese family as the nucleus in life. Nations, corporations, and other institutions are all extensions of the family and filial piety is the connecting bond. Any relationship, according to Confucius, must measure up to the father–son relationship, in which the former (father, king, employer, brother, older sister, friend) must be benevolent, just, and understanding, while the latter (son, subject, employee, younger brother, friend) must be devoted, loyal, and obedient.

Alec had grown up with the Confucian system; this foundation was not uprooted by his religious conversion to Christianity. Though his father had dismissed Alec from any family obligations, they remained in his consciousness even while living in the West under Christian ideologies. Alec and I understood that our family discussions about his mother were still being influenced by the Confucian ideals—which dictated that his older brother Raymond support their mother—though our Christian ideals asked us to give her our unconditional love and support.

***

Tensions in our family increased when my mother came from Germany to live with us. In 1979, after my father's death and her own hip fracture, my mother spent a year of recovery with us. Then, after some time back in Germany, she realized that she could no longer live alone. My mother was in her eighties at that point and I was her only child. She asked whether she might spend the rest of her life with us in the United States. In my heart there was no question that she would be welcomed and cared for—I felt deep gratitude for the stable and generous life my parents had given me—yet my mind was in terrible upheaval since we had denied Alec's mother the same option.

Accepting one's aged parent into their home was the German way, but shouldn't a Chinese parent have the same right?

We struggled with this question. Alec's parents had provided little care for him, even when they lived together. Due to business and economic problems, the Chius had sent their second son to various schools in different countries. Their desire for financial success had destroyed family intimacy. According to Confucian tradition, Raymond was responsible for their mother's care. Naturally, Alec was not happy having to justify this decision to his relatives. A gentle estrangement entered our relationship then, and I never knew whether my husband truly understood that my mother had nowhere else to live except within our home, our family, our hearts. Still I wonder if I will ever forgive myself for having been less generous toward my mother-in-law and less informed about the changes and disappointments in her life?

***

During her stay, my mother was a quiet presence in our home. She enjoyed our lifestyle as well as the company of my German-speaking friends who helped her understand aspects of American culture that she could not grasp in her limited English. She also became a member of the German Maennerchor, the oldest German organization in La Crosse.

In conversation, she often reminisced about her childhood. Her home-city of Solingen, Germany, was, and still is, famous for its cutlery industry. Her father owned a factory that produced knives. When she was sixteen her mother died, leaving her with an older sister and two brothers. She had to give up her high school studies to run the household. This was a great disappointment for her as she had liked studying and learning, but her sister was apprenticed to a dressmaker, and her brothers were working in their father's business.

When she was twenty-three she met her future husband, Heinrich Aloysius Blank, a handsome, gentle artist who had recently completed his master's training as a goldsmith. She admired his spirit and his work, and helped him develop his business after they married. In the comfortable home that had belonged to his father, they opened a studio and advertised Heinrich's craft in designing and repairing jewelry. His work quickly attracted customers and orders from larger, city shops.

When I was born, I entered a warm, loving, creative family and community. My mother encouraged my schooling and eventually directed my interest toward a degree in education from the University of Cologne. When I moved to the United States to study, and then stayed and married, my parents felt a deep loss but they never criticized or complained. America was not completely foreign to my mother. One of her brothers had immigrated to Chicago, and her father had exported many of his German cutlery products to the United States. Also, my father's brother, the Jesuit priest who would officiate my wedding, had worked in the U.S. for many decades.

My mother lived with us for the last few years of her life. She helped out around the house and garden, and served as a confidant to our teenaged children. She knew that some hard feelings had occurred because we had not allowed Alec's mother the same privilege, but when Mrs. Chiu came to visit for a few weeks the two ladies developed a good understanding as far as their different languages allowed.

My mother suffered a heart attack and died in 1981. I remain deeply grateful for my husband's support during those years, for welcoming my mother, and for sharing me and our family life with her, and the joys of her grandchildren. His tolerance was a great gift.

Once, when she was in the hospital, she said to me, "Du bist ein gutes Kind," (You are a good child), which is a remark that warms my heart to this day, reflecting that my care and love for her had started within her own heart.

My mother visiting me and Alec.

CHAPTER 26

THE EMPTYING NEST

Marcel was the first to leave for college. We soon missed his quiet manners and his help painting the apartments that Alec managed for extra income to cover the kids' college tuitions. For Marcel, the work was a means to earn extra pocket money since his tuition was free.

As the kids moved away one by one for college, graduate school, internships, and work, we rejoiced in their successes and visited them in distant places. We rode the Greyhound bus to visit Marcel in Philadelphia, where he was studying at La Salle University, and saw some of the monuments of early American history for the first time. We were surprised to see Marcel follow our own professional choices: teaching. After he finished his master's degree in science education, he was offered a teaching position in a New Jersey high school.

We visited Monica in Binghamton, New York, and with our second visit to the East Coast we gained further understanding of early American history. After earning her master's degree, she worked for Yamatake Honeywell in Japan, developing their English language business publications and teaching English. During her three years in Japan, her stories of her life there reminded Alec of his own experiences with Japanese education and culture, and encouraged his further reflection on those times. She would later go on to a doctorate in English from Emory University and also enter the teaching profession.

Ursula and Alec on the banks of the Mississippi River.

Alec with the Baums.

Michael earned his bachelor's degree at the University of Minnesota, and then worked for Ford Motor Company in Arizona. We visited Michael there and explored some of that state's natural beauties, including Lake Havasu. In a few years, he would marry Maren and attend MIT for his master's and Ph.D. in engineering.

Family photo for Michael's wedding.

Alec with Maren and Michael, Christmas 1994.

Like most of our friends, we now had an empty nest. I had retired from teaching Special Education, and Alec was still fully occupied with his teaching at Viterbo College, now University. Alec loved to listen to classical music in his office, and had close to one hundred tapes that he had recorded. Mozart was his favorite, and he watched *Amadeus,* the movie released in 1984, seven times.

I had been meeting with a group of writer-friends for several years, and writing children's stories. The support and enthusiasm of our leader, Annette White-Parks, encouraged me to eventually write my memoir during this period of semi-retirement. It took several years, but I finished and printed it with Alec's encouragement.

Alec began taking on more intricate woodworking projects with our neighbor and friend, Joe Motivans. These projects also led to larger repair work in the rentals that we managed for our family and for Raymond.

I also learned to share Alec's appreciation for the "life of wood" and its malleability as raw material for artistic designs. On our trips together, we searched for galleries selling wood products and brought home containers and vases formed of spalted wood and shaped on the lathe. At Christmas, Alec presented me with a two-foot gift box containing a carving of an avocet with a long, delicate beak on a smooth body. It is my most elegant piece of art in the living room. On a medical trip to Rochester, we added two ducks carved of cherry wood. They felt cool to the touch, with only wood grain hinting at feathers. On a later duck purchase, we appreciated wood-burning techniques that imitated a soft, feathery body cover.

Both Alec and I liked unpainted wood sculptures that used the outward form and internal design of the wood, finished with an oil rub to close the grain. Only once did Alec give me a painted bird, a cardinal, my favorite because the live ones bring happiness with their joyful colors and penetrating songs.

My interest in carved birds led me to the Center for Wood-craft in La Crosse. Elmer Grassman, a school principal, and long-time member of the Center, offered to give me an intro-duction to bird carving. Always helpful and practical, he sent inter-school mail with bird-blanks and carving instructions. He continued this training until I was ready to join the Center, where I found my classmates and instructors to be observant, patient, very kind, and supportive. Alec had experienced this before, and I was learning it then.

I was less enthusiastic about Norwegian flat-plane carving, which uses soft, but grainless, basswood. With this technique we learned to carve Santas, rural comic characters, and tree decorations that all had to be painted when completed. I never reached a level of perfection in this carving style. Unpainted birds remained my primary interest: smooth with flowing body features. Among those, I produced a woodcock and two sandpipers that I gave to friends with much pride. These were followed by life-sized ducks and a goose for my children. Mike still has his exhibited in his cabinet with glass doors.

When the nationally famous carver, Bob Guge, advertised a workshop in Burlington, Iowa, Alec suggested I take the opportunity to learn from a known artist. I was a lower-level apprentice only, but Alec, kind and sensitive as always, wanted me to take advantage of this special chance to improve my skills. He knew how encouraging progress would be for me. Together we drove down the Great River Route on a weekend, appreciating sights and time away from everyday life. I registered for the expensive course, and Alec secured two nights at a motel. "I will study while you are in class," he said, "and at night I'll share dinner with your group."

The class had only five other participants, all well-experienced carvers who gathered in a Burlington shop for wood, tools, and a wide array of carving supplies. The students were also experienced users of electric dremels, which Alec had only recently bought for me. Mr. Guge produced pre-cut basswood blanks for a life-sized killdeer. "I have seen them along the river," I mumbled, and hurried to follow the master's instructions, given in ten to fifteen minute intervals. While we worked on the assigned detail, I realized that I was slower than the rest of the group. When it came to the dremel technique, I had no experience at all. I received help here and there, but the master did not slow down his teaching, and I did not quite relax during the quick pace of the classroom. Why did I want to carve a killdeer, anyway? I wondered.

On the second day, when it came to painting, I could not use my cheap, Kmart watercolors, but had to buy a bunch of acrylic paints in the supply shop that hosted the class. The paints, along with some needed drill heads, wood glue, and glass eyes ran close to $100. I managed the painting with more joy and learned valuable techniques, such as how to fit a pair of bird eyes and how to mount the bird as a decoy on a stick, inserted into a knoll of ironwood.

I was so proud when I could show Alec the completed piece, even though the teacher had apprised apprentices like me of techniques needing further development. The class was straining, but a very worthwhile experience. Alec had treasured the quiet time at the motel and some strolls along the river. When driving home from Burlington, we calculated the expenses of this venture, and realized the bird creation amounted to almost $500! Even today, however, I proudly show my interested guests the expensive Killdeer carving.

***

Our family nest had emptied as our children went out into the world to fulfill their dreams and would eventually begin families of their own. In the meantime, Alec and I filled our nest with birds of wood.

There are still times when I look through my wood and tool boxes and rediscover finished foundations for future birds routered in oak, butternut, and walnut. I handle them gently, remembering that Alec used the router rather nervously and with great care, wanting me to have sufficient supplies for the years he could no longer help me.

Wood and tools are waiting. When will new birds emerge with joyful songs, in honor of the one who treasured and shared the craft with me?

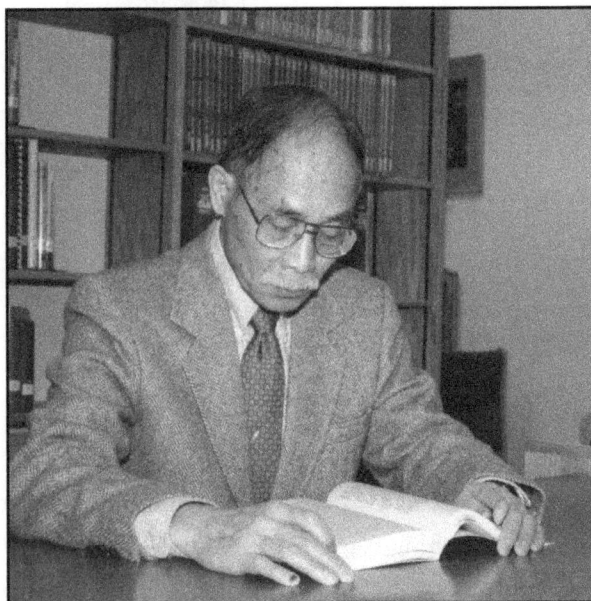

CHAPTER 27

ALEC'S RELUCTANT FAREWELL

Alec's physical health began to decline even further and he needed frequent medical attention, not only for his spinal pain but also for serious digestive problems. In the summer of 1989, Alec complained to his physician about some intestinal pains, and cancer was discovered, which eventually led to an operation to remove cancerous tissue in his colon. Alec thought he was too young to yield to cancer, and engaged in an intense exercise regimen along with controlled medication and healthier food choices, all while continuing to teach. A second operation showed that the cancer had spread and could no longer be controlled medically.

At the beginning, Alec seemed matter-of-fact about his illness, but Marcel remembers him saying, "Here I have saved so much toward a comfortable retirement, and now I will not even reach my retirement." He had planned to retire the next year. Not only would he miss the period of relaxation at the end of a demanding work life but he would not see his children advance in their professions or start families of their own. He had guided them, but had also given them the freedom to choose their own professions: Marcel had selected the sciences; Monica pursued language, literature, and writing; and Michael prepared for a career in engineering. They each were on their way.

After the terminal diagnosis, Raymond and Masako visited from Taiwan to Alec's great surprise and joy. With much eagerness, Alec and Raymond revisited the experiences of their youth. They discussed in depth their father's failed business ventures and escape to Brazil. Most importantly, Alec was able to thank Raymond for his on-going concern, support, and understanding when nobody else was able to care for him as a boy. Alec's respect and gratitude toward his brother had never ended and now found expression.

Marcel remembers accompanying the brothers to the airport, where he saw tears in Raymond's eyes during the final farewell. Shortly after this visit, Alec took to bed, refusing most of his food, and became very quiet under the influence of much morphine.

A day without pain.

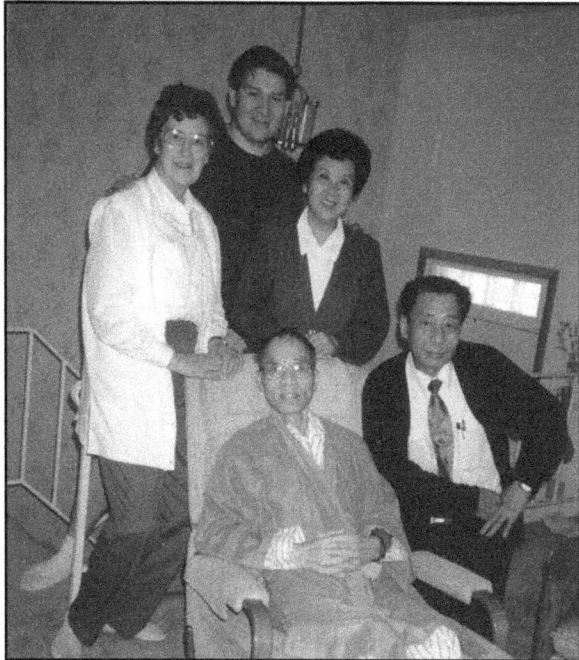

Raymond and Masako's last visit with Alec.

I was very happy that Alec was granted this personal closure with his family from Taiwan after so many years of separation, struggle, and misunderstanding. But at the end it is I, his wife of thirty-two years, who was fully blessed with Alec's companionship, consideration, and his creative and sensitive approach to our lives together that I remember with deep gratitude and love.

Marcel, Monica, and I were at his bedside when Alec's generous soul left this world quietly on July 15, 1995.

Alec, all those who have known you as son, brother, husband, father, or friend are grateful to have had you in their lives.

WALKING TO THE ONALASKA SPILLWAY

Dear Alec, *in memoriam*

Today, July 15, 1998, is the third anniversary of your death. I visit your favorite fishing spot at the Onalaska Spillway, hoping to sense your presence and feel the joy you experienced during your quiet fishing hours at this place.

You loved this river, the challenge of fishing it, and the soothing effects of water, sunshine, and wind on the body and mind. Seated on your choice rock by the dam, you clasped your fishing line, and dismissed the puzzlement of your philosophical mind and the ongoing anxieties of an immigrant's life.

At the river you could experience the single-mindedness suggested by your favorite Zen saying: "Do what you are doing!" You could devote yourself, with all your faculties, to your present moment. Relish the NOW and hold it in your hand, gently and lovingly, like the fish you pulled out, but did not want to possess.

I liked to see you return from your personal fishing spot at the spillway, refreshed and bubbling over, either with excitement over the "big one" you could prepare for dinner, or voicing disappointment over the ones who got away or simply were not there.

Today, on my way to the dam, I park at the same spot where we always left the Toyota and assembled our fishing gear. From there I walk the path along the railroad tracks. It leads across the elevated rail bed and trestle to the rocky downhill slope ending at the massive walls of the dam. The path, just two feet wide, is no longer hospitable to lonely walkers. I have to brush aside the bluish stems of wild grasses hindering my hesitant steps. With eyes on the ground, I walk slowly. I watch a bee tasting the white clover underneath the tough stems of Canadian rye and dusty sage. Why does his restless flight avoid the larger, more attractive, red clover blossoms? Are the flower tunnels too deep for his proboscis? As my eyes search uphill, to the taller growths on the slope, I wonder why bees are not also hovering around the proliferate Queen Anne's Lace. I check to see if their umber heads still display the one purple mini blossom on the flat white plane of their faces. Maybe they are meant as lures for other insects.

As I push my way through the lush assembly of wayside grasses, dusty from the passing trains, lilac phlox and tender sumac twigs with orange-tinged leaves nod from the middle tier of the slope. Even though they are homes for the chirping crickets, I brush them aside to reach the entrance to the spillway. As I walk along, I smile to myself when I remember the on-going "pull" between us: me wanting "to smell the flowers" and you urging us on to where the fish were waiting.

Before I reach the railroad crossing and the descent toward the dam, a train whistle sounds its warning and alerts me to the slow approach of the Santa Fe freight train. Soon it towers above my path on the elevated train bed, moving along slowly, on a narrow strip of land between path and river. The train's double-stacked containers dwarf life around them and throw threatening shadows over me, the fragile human of living flesh and blood. I wait until the looming boxes of unfeeling iron have passed and leave open the spot where my path crosses the tracks.

Alec, remember, we so often climbed across this pile of rocks that support the iron rails. There was no other way to reach the entrance to the dam. You used to slow down your strides toward the water to help me across the irregularities of the stones. You never forgot that my gait became strained and hesitant after I had broken my femur.

On our last walk to the dam in April 1995 we carried no fishing gear with us. It was not fishing season yet. We were there just to see how the construction work on the dam was progressing. I thought a visit to the spot where you had been so happy would make you forget for a while the discomfort of chemotherapy and the threat of the spreading cancer. Beyond the tracks, we found the entrance to the dam protected by a new fence and inaccessible to visitors.

As I sit here now, on the sleek spillway concrete wall, I realize that you would not be happy about the dam's new stream-lined construction. Designed by an efficient engineer, it has become a massive concrete incline along which the overflow of the Mississippi runs in a thin watery sheet. Gone are the big irregular rocks that once formed ledges for laying out fishing equipment. Equally gone are the square rocks at waters' edge, which provided seats close to "your" fishing hole. You always selected the same spot, where the water fell from a higher level and in swirling motion pulled the stunned fish toward your waiting hook.

I picture you on your rock, patiently casting and watching the bobber. You are in your own element, happy and carefree, and near me. The sun is glistening on the fast moving foamy waters. The heat is warming, but soothed by a gentle breeze. Beyond the cascading, swirling water, the river is calmer but still dances in little waves that reflect the sunshine. Following their movements, my mind releases hold on daily concerns that simply dissolve into intangible nothings.

Did you absorb your patience from the calming effect of the water? You never refused to thread everybody's worms or to retrieve entangled bait. Every summer you had to teach me again how to cast a line and knot the hooks and sinkers. You did not even protest when I swung the line into a tree or when the hook got stuck in my scalp and needed to be cut out by Dr. Murphy. You overlooked the children's restlessness and rejoiced with the boys, Marcel and Michael, when they finally caught the big one, while Monica sat on her favorite stone and read. Every summer you fondly reminisced that as a result of your first lesson on the rudiments of fishing, I had pulled out a painted turtle at Star Lake, near Chicago.

At this new dam, now at least, you no longer have to complain about the many Hmong fishermen who come out daily with their families or to catch fish for dinner. You were furious when the "foreigners" disregarded fishing etiquette and cast into the same hole from which you had just extracted the big walleye. I can still hear you mumble under your breath, "These damn Orientals have taken over my fishing hole."

Today only five Hmong men are fishing along the new spillway, while their small boys catch minnows for their dads. The restructured dam provides only a narrow ledge from which to reach the fish trapped in the overflow or hiding in the crannies of submerged rocks. The new dam is not "your" dam any longer. You had to find new fishing grounds in a different world.

Today, on your third anniversary of death, I feel I am near you. I know you once felt such contentment looking across this water, exposed to sun and wind, waiting for a fish to share with those who were dear to you. I know I have not lost you. You have merged with the movement of the river to its source and left me this place to visit, to reminisce and to soothe my soul when it wants to drown in sadness.

As I yield my feelings to the flowing, dancing, and whirling waters, I am reminded of Siddhartha's* dream by the river in which he gained consciousness of the unity of all life and of the relationships of all things to one another. At a fleeting moment I also feel the presence of what was and is yet to come. I, too, will be pulled by the waters of life into the Great Ocean at the end...close to the place you already know.

* Hesse, Hermann. *Siddhartha.* New York: Farrar, Strauss & Giroux, Inc., 1963.

WE REMEMBER ALEC
Thoughts expressed by friends and colleagues

My sincerest sentiments of sympathy and the assurance of my prayers for Alec's eternal rest and for the intentions of your family. As chancellor of Viterbo College, I express to you and your children my profound esteem for Alec and my gratitude for his 33 years of outstanding teaching at Viterbo College. It gives me great pleasure to know that Viterbo College has established the Alec Chiu Endowment Fund for Faculty Development in recognition of Alec's outstanding contribution to Viterbo...

(Most Rev. Raymond L. Burke, Bishop of La Crosse)

"The Gift of Self"—Presence is identified as a gift of self; the personal conveyance of a sincere desire to understand; attending physically, spiritually and emotionally to another person. In the words of Gabriel Marcel, presence "refreshes my inner being, reveals me to myself, makes me more fully myself." Presence is not only "being there" or "being there with," it is also "being there for." Presence creates a freeing space, a nurturing ambiance, a solidarity, a communion, a connectedness without which stagnation occurs. With presence the work of spirit continues... We honor and appreciate the presence of Alec Chiu by establishing the Alec Chiu Faculty Award.

(Dr. William Medland, President, Viterbo College)

We have worked many years together. I have always respected you as a person, as an educator and as a colleague. You always challenged your students to go beyond the superficial, to think critically and to read critically. Our legacy as educators — if we are good at what we do — is that we can change people's lives for the better. You were a good teacher, and I know you had a significant input on many students, and on me, your colleague. I will miss you a great deal. As you face this difficult journey, you must know that we love you and will miss you. You did good work at Viterbo.

(Dr. Michael Collins, Colleague at Viterbo)

To Dr. Alec Chiu, You were one of less than a handful of professors who shaped my thinking at Viterbo and the U.W. Madison. Thank you! ... You allowed and encouraged me to read Existential Philosophy — as well as all Philosophy. What I appreciated most was you; your sharing of experiences and personal insights. I was your student in two Philosophy and one Economics class — early 1960. The recent article in the Viterbo magazine spoke of your illness, but also of your joys; Ursula and your children. When Marcel was a baby we all had to look at him in the Library. Monica was just born, when I graduated. Since then I have left the convent, married a Biblical scholar and adopted two children. I completed my Ph. D. in Educational Philosophy, and since then have specialized in education of the gifted and talented for whom I wrote the enclosed text, Philosophy and Philosophers. I wrote this program so that young people could have the advantage of Philosophy, as well as the "tools" to help them in life.

(Lois F. Roetz, Ed.D., student at the beginning of Alec's career)

Dear Dr. Chiu, Some of your wisdom rubbed off on me, and I have often thought of things you taught me in my exchanges with others. In this manner the knowledge you possessed has been translated. With highest respect and admiration,

(Julian Wheat, student)

I had you as a teacher at Viterbo for a couple of Philosophy classes. I want to thank you for what I have learned through your wisdom, and I want you to know that you are in my thoughts. I am thankful that I had the chance to meet you.

(Stacey Mitby, student)

Alec had the willpower and courage of a giant! He fought a good fight and now — he is in peace.

(Anna Motivans, family friend)

We always enjoyed his wit and humor. I especially remember the good times Alec, Joe Motivans and I had in the cabinet-making classes at WWTC. I also remember the fun we had at a Summer picnic Alec had for men in your backyard. I feel a deep loss with both Alec and Joe Motivans gone. They were my good friends.

(Dr. Charles Haas, friend)

I want you to know how much Alec was appreciated by the Viterbo College family. He will be sadly missed by everyone who had the good fortune to know him. His contribution to Viterbo cannot be measured, except by the tremendous legacy of his BEING and his contribution to higher education.

(Sister Annarose Glum, Viterbo Music Faculty)

We both have such fond memories of the times we spent with you and Alec. We count as a treasure the lovely vase Alec made. He was such an intelligent, able man with a wonderful sense of humor. We will miss him.

(Maureen & Bruce Knutson, neighbors)

I had the pleasure of working with Alec on several committees at Viterbo. His keen insights, dedication and genuine respect for all will be deeply missed.

(Michael Smutska, Viterbo administration)

I will always consider my acquaintance and friendship with Alec to be a special honor. And this was enhanced with my attendance and participation in the memorial Mass, Tuesday afternoon.

(Jeanne Linderbaum, Registrar, Viterbo)

I will always remember how close our families were when we were growing up. My photo albums are full of pictures at the farm and at the Lake — and always we begged for Alec to please make his special grilled chicken wings — in his "secret sauce", of course. Such wonderful memories for all six of Motivans children.

(Sylvia Motivans-Pocs, daughter of family friend)

In the short time I spent with you and Alec it was easy to see the love and respect you held for one another.

(Dick and Carol, neighbors)

Alec's passing will certainly leave a great void for all of us at Viterbo. He will be greatly missed.

(Jan Koppelman, Academic Media, Viterbo)

You know that I grieve deeply with you, but also rejoice that Alec is now enjoying the Source of Life and all that is good. The enclosed is a small contribution to the Alec Chiu Endowment Fund for Faculty Development. It makes me happy to know he will be remembered in this way. This little note card (depicting Chinese Angel fish) is in memory of Alec as a true Chinese fisherman. The Liturgy yesterday was a wonderful celebration of LIFE. Thank you for the part each of you carried out. Alec is now even more proud of his family, if that's possible.

(Sister Grace, former Viterbo President who hired Alec in 1963)

We will remember Alec with appreciation for his fine spirit…
which lives in you and all of us who knew him.

(Keith & Lynne Valiquette, friends)

I wanted to express to you the deep respect and admiration that I
have for you as a person, a teacher , and a friend. The courage that
you displayed this semester will never be forgotten. Some people
feel that there are no heroes left today, but I disagree. You are a
hero; truly inspirational. I am honored to be your student, and I
want you to know that I do have a very great appreciation for the-
oretical knowledge and for life. Thank you for the greatest lesson
any one could learn in Philosophy: to follow through with what
you believe. You are so special!

(Nancy Ziegeweit, student)

Alec had a profound influence on all of us who were fortunate
enough to be his colleagues. He will not soon be forgotten. Alec's
thoughtfulness, integrity and intelligence were a force in his deal-
ings with us. I will miss him a great deal and so sense some measure
of your loss.

(Mary & Mike Collins, colleague)

Your Delta, Kappa Gamma Sisters have held you in their thoughts
and prayers during the long illness of your scholarly and talented
husband. He has touched the hearts of so many students, neighbors
and of his family.

(Pauline Abel, President Delta, K. G. Society)

I knew Alec only through you and several of his friends. He truly was a remarkable man.

(Pat Hiebert, friend)

We plan to purchase a Japanese flowering crabapple tree to be planted on the campus of Viterbo College in Alec's honor. He will live on in our hearts and memories.

(Ron Amel, Jim Larson, Jim Lawrence, colleagues)

Alec was not only my colleague; he was also my friend. In all my conversations with him his main concern was always his wife and each of his children. I grieve that this great and good man will not be here to steady us with his single-mindedness and his large-hearted humor.

(Sister Laurian Pieterek, colleague in Philosophy)

I have always valued the times both of you stimulated me with your conversation. He has contributed much to society.

(Mary Morse, widow of a colleague)

I wish I had known your husband better. He was a wonderful man and your outstanding family is a tribute to him.

(Sue Pelton, children's elementary school teacher)

Alec, indeed, meant a lot to many people. We are blessed that he touched our lives.

(Lon & Linda Ziehm, friends)

I am grateful to have met Alec, talked to him and to have known him enough to admire his grace, his dignity, his fortitude — and his many talents. It is a great loss to the Viterbo College community. May his spirit awaken in God's grace. Death is a part of life. It has its mystery, hence, beauty. As Gertrude says to Hamlet; " All that lives must die."

(Dr. Lalita Pandit, University of Wisconsin)

Both my wife and I had the privilege to learn from the teaching and interactions with Mr. Chiu. I enjoyed, and more importantly, I recognized the positive effect that I experienced when taking philosophy courses with Mr. Chiu. Besides the intellectual growth that I experienced during his classes, I remember the sense of respect that he consistently showed towards me. And lastly, I remember the sense of personal discipline that he nurtured in his interactions with students. I have many positive feelings about my educational and personal experiences at Viterbo College. I can honestly say that my experiences with Mr. Chiu stand out as one of my more nurturing ones while at Viterbo College, and indicative of the values of a liberal education. May the seeds of his dedicated work with his students bring him and his loved ones many rewards.

(Jerry DeBoer, former student)

Dear Alec Chiu, Dec. 7, 1994

I want to thank you for presenting one of the most interesting and informative courses that I have ever had the pleasure of participating in. Though the subject matter was interesting, it was the thought provoking way in which you presented it, and resulting discussion which made Philosophy 101 the highlight of my academic year. I thank you for a class in which I was made to think instead of memorize and understand instead of accept. I thank you for a course that changes the way I see the world, and not just the way I name the things in it. I also thank your wife for her critique of my history reports which was in harmony with the rest of this invigorating course.

(Will Kilkeary)

Dear Dad,

It's wonderful to have you as a supportive father. I am glad I could come home and celebrate your birthday (3/10/95) with you, and especially enjoy your stories and photos of the past. You are truly a hero through all your travels and your suffering. I have much respect and Love for you.

(Monica, daughter)

Alec visiting Mt. Fuji.

Raymond (l) and one of his sons (mid), and Alec (r).

Alec (r) visiting his family in Taiwan.

One of our many fishing adventures together.

Alec Chiu.

www.ingramcontent.com/pod-product-compliance
Lightning Source LLC
LaVergne TN
LVHW011158080426
835508LV00007B/466